# [Re]inventing
# the Wheel

# [Re]inventing the Wheel

## Advancing the Dialogue on Contemporary American Indian Art

Nancy J. Blomberg, editor

DENVER ART MUSEUM

# Contents

Fig. 1      *Trade Canoe for Don Quixote,* 2004
Jaune Quick-to-See Smith
Mixed media on canvas, 60 × 200 in.

The Denver Art Museum (DAM) has a long history of honoring American Indian arts and cultures through a combination of its large and exceptional collections, innovative public programs, and scholarly publications. Our collections represent nearly every native culture from Alaska to Florida, all time periods from ancient Eskimo ivories to Jaune Quick-to-See Smith's haunting 2004 *Trade Canoe for Don Quixote* (Fig. 1), and all artistic traditions, including sculpture, weaving, ceramics, and painting. By combining this incredibly rich heritage of native artistic creativity with curatorial and scholarly passion, the DAM has placed American Indian arts squarely within the framework of our collections from Europe, Asia, Africa, America, and the South Pacific for more than eighty years.

Frederic Douglas, one of the museum's first curators, was a groundbreaker in the field of museology. His efforts—not only in Denver, but also at the 1939 World's Fair, the 1941 *Indian Art of the United States* exhibition at the Museum of Modern Art, his American Indian fashion

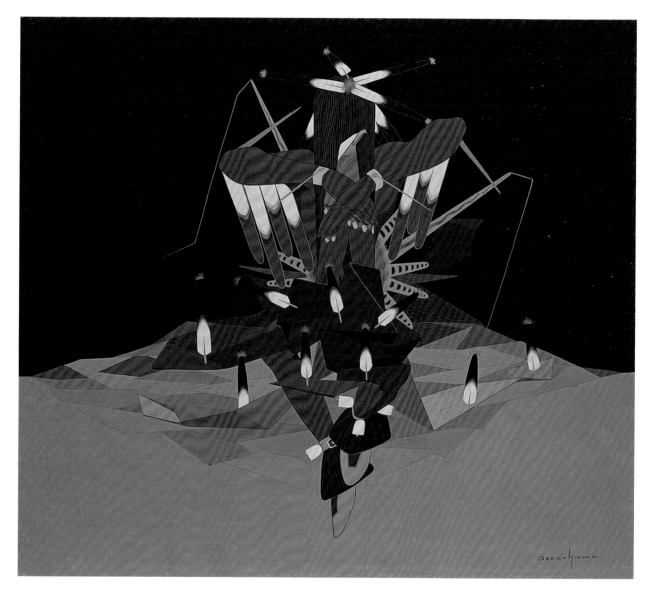

Fig. 2    *Sioux Eagle Dancer,* 1954
          Oscar Howe
          Casein and dammar on paper, 20 × 22½ in.

shows of the 1940s and 1950s, and his contemporary painting shows in the early 1950s (where we acquired our extraordinary Oscar Howe paintings [Fig. 2])—raised national and international awareness of the rich art forms created by American Indian artists.

While the greatest strengths of our American Indian collection are historic, current collecting priorities by curators Nancy Blomberg and Polly Nordstrand have extended the early collections by focusing on the finest expressions of contemporary artists, such as Jolene Rickard's installation *Corn Blue Room* (frontispiece); Harry Fonseca's magical painting *Shuffle Off to Buffalo #V* (Fig. 3); and the monumental sculpture *Wheel,* by HOCK E AYE VI Edgar Heap of Birds, which precipitated the "[Re]inventing the Wheel" symposium and this publication. Contemporary trends and practices in creating art have likewise brought about changes in how curators and scholars interpret these artworks and raised critical questions addressed in this book.

Funding for "[Re]inventing the Wheel" was provided by an Economic Development Initiative grant made possible by former U.S. Senator Ben Nighthorse Campbell with additional funding provided by the citizens who support the Scientific and Cultural Facilities District. Publication and distribution of this book were generously underwritten by the Ford Foundation with the support and encouragement of Elizabeth Theobald Richards. Enormous thanks to all for helping us to convene this important group of artists and scholars to enrich our understanding of American Indian arts and debate some of the critical issues of our time.

Lewis I. Sharp
Frederick and Jan Mayer Director
Denver Art Museum

SHUFFLE OFF TO BUFFALO *V*
BY
HARRY FONSECA

# Acknowledgments

Convening a distinguished group of scholars to spend a day debating key issues in the field of Native American art today is a rewarding and stimulating intellectual exercise. Translating that lively discussion into a printed volume is the work of many, many people.

Initial funds to develop the symposium were provided by an Economic Development Initiative grant made possible by former U.S. Senator Ben Nighthorse Campbell with additional funding provided by the citizens who support the Scientific and Cultural Facilities District. This publication has been generously supported by a multiyear grant from the Ford Foundation with the strong endorsement of Elizabeth Theobald Richards. The film *Inciting Memory: The Creative Process of HOCK E AYE VI Edgar Heap of Birds* was made possible by a Scientific and Cultural Facilities District Millennium grant.

Within the Denver Art Museum, the Development Department, led by Jennifer Darling and including Megan Cooke, manager of foundation relations, has worked hard to make these grants possible. In our Photography Department, Jeff Wells and Christina Jackson ably converted slides to print-format images. Julie Wilson in the New World Department and Angelica Daneo, assistant curator in the Painting and Sculpture Department, offered advice and guidance on the publication process.

The staff of the Native Arts Department worked tirelessly to bring this book to print. Jennifer Pray, curatorial assistant, managed the enormous project of securing high-quality images and associated permission rights for all the beautiful works illustrated in this book. Associate curator Polly Nordstrand, in addition to being one of the key authors, was a driving force in both the symposium and working with the publisher, essayists, and artists to make this a significant contribution to a changing field.

Special thanks and kudos go to Laura Caruso, our editor, who patiently received manuscripts from seven different authors and expertly crafted them into a cohesive whole while retaining the style and voice of each one.

To all the authors—many thanks for being willing to contribute your time, energy, and unique insights into advancing this dialogue.

To anyone who has been inadvertently omitted, my apologies—and sincere thanks.

Nancy J. Blomberg
Curator of Native Arts

Fig. 3    *Shuffle Off to Buffalo #V,* 1983
Harry Fonseca
Acrylic and mixed media on canvas, 60 × 48 in.

# Introduction

## Advancing the Dialogue

*by Nancy J. Blomberg*

In 1996 the physical and intellectual landscape at the Denver Art Museum was on the verge of change. For nearly a century, the museum's curators had pursued an often-groundbreaking agenda to collect and promote the work of American Indian artists. Now curatorial staff was proposing an even bolder statement—commissioning a major public sculpture by a living American Indian artist for the front entrance of the museum. While visitors were long accustomed to interior galleries and scholarly publications celebrating American Indian art, a monumental work of public art would unequivocally signal to all who passed by that American Indian art was the flagship collection at the DAM, and that American Indian artists were an integral part of the best of world art. And so the search began . . .

A number of sculptors experienced in creating outdoor art were contacted and asked to submit preliminary proposals for a large space adjacent to the main entrance. The artists were not given any limitations other than the physical constraints of the site, roughly seventy-five feet in diameter, and consideration for the harsh extremes of Denver weather in the selection and use of materials. We privately hoped for a sculpture that would be site-specific not only in terms of size, shape, and materials but also in intellectual content—a sculpture that would be not only beautiful but thought-provoking and engaging.

We received many wonderful submissions and wish we could have acquired them all. In the end, however, it was the proposal by HOCK E AYE VI Edgar Heap of Birds that most excited us with all of its complexities. It was not only the perfect artistic and architectural form for the site, but the intellectual content embedded in the sculpture was uniquely relevant to Denver. It re-examined the past but looked to the future as well. Through powerful text and imagery, *Wheel* (Fig. 4) specifically addressed the history of Indian peoples in Colorado from Heap of Birds's perspective as a Cheyenne-Arapaho artist whose ancestors have

Fig. 4 *Wheel,* 2005
Edgar Heap of Birds
Porcelain on steel, diam. 50 ft.

had a long and often painful history in the region—as well as from the multiple perspectives of other Indian tribes who have lived in Colorado for centuries. We envisioned it as an active and vital space where groups could come together for community and personal renewal and as a community gathering place to celebrate or commemorate important historical events (as is the case with the Sand Creek Massacre Spiritual Healing Run, held each year on the anniversary of the Sand Creek massacre). We hoped that it would stimulate both public dialogue and private contemplation. And, lastly, we saw *Wheel* as an important teaching tool to build bridges between the diverse groups of people who live in and visit Denver.

The installation of *Wheel* has garnered much attention —both positive and negative—and has raised many questions specifically about this artwork and more broadly about the nature of both public art and contemporary Indian art. With *Wheel* itself boldly suggesting new interpretations of American history, we asked ourselves what should our roles be as curators, scholars, critics, and artists to advance a dialogue in positive and meaningful ways? Commissioning *Wheel* was an important moment for the DAM that has served as a catalyst for future action—in particular, the initiation of a biennial symposium series examining critical issues in contemporary American Indian art. The inaugural symposium was held January 28, 2006; drawing inspiration from *Wheel,* we titled it "[Re]inventing the Wheel." This book is yet another spin-off of *Wheel.* Using *Wheel* and the work of Edgar Heap of Birds as a starting point, noted scholars in the field present critical new thinking about the complex social and artistic issues surrounding Native American art today.

The public art projects created by Heap of Birds have embraced a variety of physical and political landscapes around the world. Heap of Birds's contribution to this publication is that of an artist painting a very personal portrait of his career, beginning with his early days and concluding with the complexities of *Wheel,* his first large-scale permanent installation as well as his biggest project to date. His intimate look at his aspirations and motivations touches on his family, his university studies, his international travels, his many collaborations, and his engagement with political events, and how each has shaped his life and his art.

Jackson Rushing's paper presents a formal analysis of *Wheel* and other work by Heap of Birds. This analysis looks at Heap of Birds's work in the context of other postmodern artists who investigate "the complex relationship between language, 'reality,' and power." By closely examining the structure and meaning of Heap of Birds's art, Rushing builds his case to position Heap of Birds squarely in the center of work by such renowned international artists as Maya Lin, whose powerful public art projects like the Vietnam Veterans Memorial also "investigate history and give form to traumatic memory"—an excellent example of contextualization within a broader art historical framework.

## Defining and Positioning American Indian Art

*There is no way to see his [Heap of Birds] work as "ethnic," as "Indian art"; but there is no way to escape the Indian reality his work represents.*
—Jimmie Durham[1]

We've used *Wheel* as a stimulus for a more critical consideration of issues in the field today—issues that have been debated and contested and have threatened to divide artists, curators, scholars, and critics whose lives have been completely enmeshed in something we call "American

Indian art." But what exactly is "Indian" art? It's certainly not a new question, and I'm not the first to ask it—as evidenced by a lifetime in the field plus a quick search of the literature. In 1959, participants at the Rockefeller Conference at the University of Arizona addressed this very question, and many distinguished artists and scholars in the nearly half-century since then have likewise offered opinions. In 1975 prominent artist T. C. Cannon issued his famous statement:

> First of all, let me say that an Indian painting is any painting that's done by an Indian. Today, however, I don't think there is such a thing as an "Indian painting." There are so many modes that people are working in that it seems beside the point to call a painting Indian just because the artist is an Indian. People don't call a work by Picasso a Spanish painting, they call it a Picasso. After all, Picasso spent most of his time in France anyway. Does that make him a Spanish painter or a French painter? I say it makes him Picasso.[2]

To some it may seem an irrelevant question—or one with an obvious answer, as in this oft-quoted comment made by Cannon more than three decades ago. However, the question only hints at the real issue. For decades now, scholars and artists have lamented the lack of acceptance/inclusion of American Indian art in the mainstream, and they have debated the language of the criticism of that art with no seeming answers.

So, back to the original question: Is it a valid, identifiable category? If it is, then how should it be collected and displayed in museums, art galleries, and international art fairs? What kind of discussion and critique would propel it into a more prominent presence in the art world? (Of course the flip side of those questions is, if it is *not* a valid, identifiable category, do we dare ask: what then?)

In 1961, Frederick Dockstader, director of the Heye Foundation's Museum of the American Indian in New York, said that Indian art could not be defined except by "basic racial origin."[3] Thirty-five years later scholar Charlotte Townsend-Gault also questioned the validity of the category:

> Given the diversity of work—in history and in intent as well as appearance, Native artists being confronted with as many aesthetic choices as any others, I would say that First Nations art is not an art category at all, but a shared socio-political situation constituted by a devastating history, the powers of the Indian Act, the social geographies of the reservation system, by tribal and local politics, by the shifting demographics of the non-Native in pluralistic society, and by the worldwide ethnic revival.[4]

And then four years later Margaret Dubin offered a similar observation:

> The very existence of a cohesive field of objects capable of being gathered under the heading of Native American art is dubious. With producers hailing from more than 500 different cultural groups, not including cultures married into, any formal unity derives more from shared social and historical experiences than a pre-contact tribal aesthetic.[5]

In their beautiful 2004 book *First American Art,* Bruce Bernstein and Gerald McMaster tackled this very issue and asked whether an American Indian aesthetic exists, and if so, what are the criteria for understanding it? They answered a resounding "yes" and then outlined seven defining principles.[6] A very bold and innovative move—but to advocate for "a" Native American aesthetic is to continue to promulgate the widely held popular stereotype of

*Untitled (Bonnie and Clyde Series #3),* 1992
Mateo Romero
Oil on canvas, 40 × 60¼ in.

"the" Indian. It denies the hundreds and hundreds of tribal groups across the United States and Canada—not to mention individual artists—each with widely disparate aesthetic systems. It may be possible to describe a particular moment in time, say, a Crow aesthetic in 1875, by identifying such things as designs, colors, materials, shapes, and layout, but as any Plains scholar can attest, even that approach has limitations.

Fifty years and we're still debating . . . and asking more questions: What defines Indian art today? Is it blood quantum or subject matter? Is the topic of the art important or the identity of the artist? And what about artists who were not raised in their communities: Bill Reid, John Hoover, and Kay WalkingStick? It gets even more complex with artists such as Ed Archie Noisecat, whose art reflects the influences of many tribes. And, of course, coming back to our starting point, Edgar Heap of Birds and *Wheel*—what about a sculpture made of porcelain enamel on a steel structure, fabricated in a foundry in Dallas, Texas?

We're not really going around in circles—or are we? If the central issue is the position of this art in the greater art world then I'll ask yet another set of questions: Should we shift the dialogue from "Indian" to "art"? If yes, then how? Followed by: if not, why not?

Two chapters in this volume address this issue. In his essay, Alfred Young Man, First Nations Cree artist and anthropologist, looks at the positioning of First Nations art in Canadian museums. He argues against the current trend of incorporating First Nations art into "the postmodern mainstream," while forcefully articulating a need for "a great change of consciousness" in studying, displaying, and writing about native art. Young Man argues for an acceptance of native art on an equal footing with other art, while recognizing and celebrating its own historical movements.

Much of Nancy Mithlo's writing in recent years has tackled the issue of confronting stereotypes both inside and outside Indian communities. In a surprising twist, she examines how artists such as Jean LaMarr and Shelley Niro have incorporated negative stereotypes directly into their art "as a means of capturing their power for alternate readings." Mithlo says that this re-appropriation allows the artists to powerfully gain attention and then redirect the negative message. Concerned also with stagnation in the field of native arts in articulating a satisfactory contemporary native arts theory, Mithlo offers a model for an indigenous arts scholarship with women artists at the center.

## Breaking the Code

*The prevailing code of how Indian contemporary art should be presented . . . strongly advises that Indian artists should be in a group exhibition with other Indians. The code also advises that only Indians have authority to speak on Indian issues, and Indian issues should be about "land" or "identity" or "we are / have always been / will always be here" and that Indians are "sacred" and so forth. The proper role of a white curator is to facilitate the neutral presentation of Indian artists and their work, and to have no real opinion on the content. The proper role of white artists, well, they don't really have a role. The code has been in effect for a couple of decades now and to state things bluntly, it feels deader than disco.*

Paul Chaat Smith[7]

Paul Chaat Smith, a most forceful, lucid, and witty writer and thinker, has issued a wake-up call to the field. This quote, taken from an essay he wrote for a groundbreaking

*Cloud Stone,* 1987
Preston Duwyenie
Alabaster and copper, 45 × 21 × 11 in.

exhibition at the Aldrich Contemporary Art Museum, criticizes the prevailing "code" and lauds Aldrich curator Richard Klein for his new presentation of contemporary art.

So, why are we now well into the twenty-first century still using the unproductive rhetoric of the last century? (Are we stubborn? not very bright? fearful? or just asleep?) We are definitely a very small, inbred group of curators, artists, scholars, and critics who have a tendency to segregate ourselves and then complain about the lack of acceptance and exposure in the "mainstream." We must acknowledge our insularity, move outside our small circle, and invite new people to the table / podium / gallery.

To be fair, there has been some movement in this direction in recent years with symposiums at the Eiteljorg Museum of American Indians and Western Art (2005), the National Museum of the American Indian ("Vision, Space, Desire," 2005), and the University of Illinois ("American Art Histories and Transdisciplinary Practices," 2007) calling for a broadening of the discussion among a larger group of people. The NMAI symposium was held at the Venice Biennale and was especially notable for its deliberate selection of a wide range of participants to "voice new ideas and explore interdisciplinary frameworks" and to "produce unexpected insights and map new directions for the future."[8] Many of the participants offered critical comments supporting the goals of the symposium, including Jean Fisher ("insularity is not the way forward"), Sylvie Fortin ("we must put in place sustainable structures . . . new precise, nimble, and multiple vehicles"), and finally, returning once more to our starting point, Edgar Heap of Birds ("native artists have become insular by seeing themselves as different and therefore special"). All argued eloquently to open up the discussion to a broader base of participants in order to develop a more inclusive—and accurate—art history.[9]

Dianne Harris offered a critical observation at the University of Illinois symposium on the current state of art history as a profession by suggesting that "the ghettoization of 'other' artists has led to the ghettoization of art history itself. Art history has become an intellectual backwater. It is smaller than it should be."[10] In this book, two writers address issues of identity politics, insularity, and marginalization. Lucy R. Lippard recounts some of the multiple choices contemporary Indian artists make, for instance, between tradition and modernization, wisely pointing out that it need not be either/or, because "tradition is not the antithesis of modernism, but its mulch." In attempting to balance issues of the artists' identities with their art, Lippard chastises all of us: curators, critics, and artists for our roles in romanticizing the past.

Polly Nordstrand's insightful essay surveys exhibitions and publications on American Indian art over the past fifteen years and questions the most common assumptions expressed in each. She challenges the idea that separate shows of Indian art are crucial to bring greater visibility to Indian artists, arguing instead that such segregation perpetuates a "substandard position." She disputes the notion that Indian art must always be about survival and advocates for the writing of a new, more relevant and analytical art criticism that focuses on "the aesthetic." Frustrated by the continued ghettoization of Indian art, Nordstrand, much like Young Man, suggests identifying movements in the history of Native American art in order to understand the impact of Indian artists "as influential instead of a reaction to Western culture."

To be completely honest here, the term "Indian" has always been problematic for me as an artificial construct— assigned to others by others—to create a monolithic and homogeneous grouping that does not now, and never has, existed. If we accept American Indian art as a valid category for scholarly study, then it must no longer be studied

*Farewell to the Smokies*, 2007
Kay WalkingStick
Oil on wood panel diptych, 36 × 72 in.

*Ganondaman's Tribute to Ray,* 1996–2004
G. Peter Jemison
Mixed media on paper bag, 17 × 13¾ × 5¼ in.

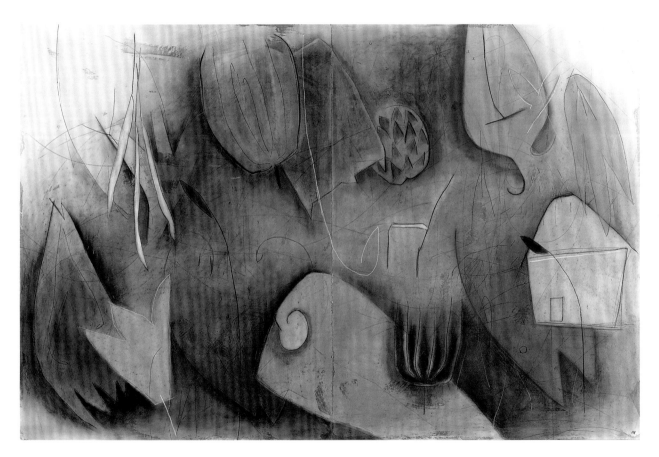

*Dreaming,* 1989
Emmi Whitehorse
Oil on paper on canvas, 50 × 76½ in.

solely in isolation—for it was never created in isolation. American Indian art did not develop in a vacuum. There were many, many influences among different tribes—and from non-Indians. We have all been complicit in a false narrative of purity, immutable tradition, and isolation. We must acknowledge and celebrate the complexities of cross-cultural exchange, because the Taos School, the Hudson River School, and the Santa Fe Studio School of artists did not develop in isolation. Our segregation of American Indian art has not raised awareness; instead we have unwittingly fragmented a common narrative to the detriment of the narrative. We need a new narrative acknowledging the roles and influences of all the participants—in all directions; a narrative that is more dynamic and a new art history that is more accurate. Tomás Ybarra-Frausto has argued for a new paradigm but cautions that it should be "neither separatist nor assimilationist but relational."[11]

Most previous organizational strategies have either been framed by the broad temporal and value-laden categories of traditional vs. contemporary or by anthropological culture area / tribal classification. Limited attempts have been made to discuss Native American art within the context of American art or world art. However, on a very positive note, Dr. Janet Catherine Berlo, noted scholar of Native American art, has just collaborated on a new college-level textbook titled *American Encounters*.[12] While it has not been released at the time of this writing, conversations with Berlo indicate that it will be a new—and more inclusive—examination of American art that situates the contributions of American Indian artists within a larger context. We can hope that this new approach will begin to break the code in positive ways and begin to stimulate critical new thinking in the next generation of art historians.

All of the writers in *[Re]inventing the Wheel* have responded to the challenge to advance the dialogue beyond the parochialism of the past—although each in different ways. The challenge to all of us is to continue this discussion in thoughtful and constructive ways. Rennard Strickland eloquently and succinctly summed up the solution to our stagnation a quarter of a century ago:

> Sound analysis of Indian art requires that disciplines join together in their work . . . More sophisticated understanding of Indian art demands the co-operative inquiry of patrons, collectors, traders, teachers, curators and the artists themselves. A reasoned evaluative perspective must be established so that current Indian art controversies do not continue forever. The debate over modernism and traditional must be brought to an end . . . Indian art should become the thoughtful study by individuals of all perspectives. No longer should Indian painting and sculpture be considered in isolation, classed alternately as ethnography or fine art or tourist curio. Only when a new perspective has been established will we begin to debate the universal aspects of Indian art . . . Only then will we understand the divergent influences of historical events and artistic developments.[13]

Are we up to the challenge?

24

# Notes

1. Jimmie Durham, "A Central Margin," in *The Decade Show: Frameworks of Identity in the 1980s* (New York: Museum of Contemporary Hispanic Art, New Museum of Contemporary Art, and Studio Museum of Harlem, 1990), 168.

2. T. C. Cannon, quoted in Jamake Highwater, *Song from the Earth: American Indian Painting* (Boston: New York Graphic Society, 1976), 177.

3. Frederick J. Dockstader, *Indian Art in America: The Arts and Crafts of the North American Indian* (Greenwich, CT: New York Graphic Society, 1961), 18.

4. Charlotte Townsend-Gault, "Translation or Perversion? Showing First Nations Art in Canada," *Cultural Studies* 9, no. 1 (1995): 94.

5. Margaret Dubin, "Sanctioned Scribes: How Critics and Historians Write the Native American Art World," in *Native American Art in the Twentieth Century,* ed. W. Jackson Rushing III (New York: Routledge, 1999), 155.

6. Bruce Bernstein and Gerald McMaster, *First American Art: The Charles and Valerie Diker Collection of American Indian Art* (Washington, DC: Smithsonian National Museum of the American Indian in association with the University of Washington Press, 2004), 10, 12.

7. Paul Chaat Smith, "Americans without Tears," in *No Reservations: Native American History and Culture in Contemporary Art,* curated by Richard Klein with essays by Fergus M. Bordewich, Paul Chaat Smith, and Richard Klein (Ridgefield, CT: Aldrich Contemporary Art Museum, 2006), 98.

8. Gerald McMaster, "New Art / New Contexts," introduction to *Vision, Space, Desire: Global Perspectives and Cultural Hybridity* (Washington, DC: National Museum of the American Indian, Smithsonian Institution, 2006), 21.

9. *Vision, Space, Desire: Global Perspectives and Cultural Hybridity.* The quotations in the text are found on the following pages: Jean Fisher, 42; Sylvie Fortin, 110; and Edgar Heap of Birds, 25.

10. University of Illinois symposium, "American Art Histories and Transdisciplinary Practices," April 2007. The quoted material is from the author's notes made at the symposium.

11. Ibid.

12. Angela Miller, Janet Berlo, Bryan Wolf, and Jennifer Roberts, *American Encounters: Art, History and Cultural Identity* (New York: Prentice Hall, 2007).

13. Rennard Strickland, "Beyond the Ethnic Umbrella: Learning More about Contemporary Indian Painting and Sculpture," in *Magic Images: Contemporary Native American Art,* ed. Edwin Wade and Rennard Strickland (Norman, OK: Philbrook Art Center and University of Oklahoma Press, 1981), 118.

Fig. 5     *Wheel*, 2005
Edgar Heap of Birds
Porcelain on steel, diam. 50 ft.

I would like to begin by acknowledging some very important elements. First, the waters located near us such as the rivers that are flowing, the lakes, the rain that comes, or the snow that is going to melt. This water is what renews us all everywhere in the world, whether it is the oceans, rivers, or lakes—all these shores we have. I want to acknowledge these waters. I also want to acknowledge the animals that are around us, below us, or flying above us (some of which you will see on *Wheel*). Of course, those animals are here not only to serve us as commodities, but to instruct us as well. If you listen to them, follow them, and understand them, then you will realize that they are helpful to us. We cannot live without them. Next, I would like to acknowledge the plants. I think all of us who come from Native communities, or even if you have your own garden in the city, know that the plants are also here to assist us. For most of us who live on the prairies east of the Rocky Mountains, we cannot live without our plants. We cannot move away from these herbs, which serve as instructors that grow out of the ground. Finally, I would like to acknowledge the mountains. The Front Range marks our reservation, the reservation of the Cheyenne and Arapaho people. I want to acknowledge the mountains because when one goes through the ceremony, they put you on the rocks and then, of course, you can touch the earth. That mountain was once a molten river. Today, it is big and tall and hard, but once it was flowing, it was molten earth. We always want to get close to those rocks, so it is good that we are close to the mountains today. I think that *Wheel* itself was created to help support this day. That is the best thing I can say about that sculpture: it is built to support what we are going to do in our lives. I think it helps us a little bit today, so I want to start with those acknowledgments.

# Life as Art
# Creating through Acts of
# Personal and Cultural Renewal
*by HOCK E AYE VI Edgar Heap of Birds*

*This essay is adapted from a talk given on January 28, 2006, by Edgar Heap of Birds at the Denver Art Museum's "[Re]inventing the Wheel" symposium.*

## Early Work: Kansas & California

I grew up in Kansas, so it was always important to me to see the horizon. I think a lot of our Native American art-work is based on the geometry of the horizon and the Earth itself (Fig. 12). As a young student in Kansas, I did not have a lot of understanding of this nomenclature, but as I look back on it, I see that what I was really doing was using the horizon line to locate my painting. In addition to painting, I also made serigraphs, which is a process similar to silk-screen. I still do a lot of prints today but more as someone who directs the printing. I would define myself as an ele-mental artist because I work with a lot of elemental issues in my art. In that way, I am okay with calling myself a modernist—I do not find it to be a dirty word.

During a break from college, I went to California and experimented with video art, holograms, and glasswork. But when I came back to Kansas, I was not focused, and I ended up making new work with material that came out of dumpsters. I totally changed my materials. It was happenstance really. I found a lot of things in a dumpster one night, then went back to my studio and made all these sculptures, or constructions, with things like a piece of cardboard that would have been used to pack up a refrig-erator (Fig. 13). In retrospect, I was influenced by the same horizon line that I had always been involved with, since it functioned as a conceptual framework that exemplified the beautiful to me. This work progressed over about a year's time. It became even more fluid to where I was using found objects like cheesecloth, fabrics, and so on. I think that experience taught me a lot about space—how one moves into a space and communicates with a space. It was important to me that the sculptural constructions have that freedom to move in space. Certainly, *Wheel* has that. All my work has that. Exhibits that I have put in museums have that. It is about being in a location and how you re-late to that location.

When I was back in college in Kansas, I befriended a very important artist, a student of Dr. Dick West at Haskell. His name was Don Secondine, a Lenni Lenape artist, who worked in the 1970s. We became friends and took a landscape painting class together. It so happened that we had an instructor who did easel painting, which we thought was pretty parochial. We thought, "We don't do that," but we went on a class field trip anyway and wound up making earthworks (Fig. 14). Don's mother-in-law had died earlier that season, so we made a memorial to her consisting of a large standing tree with cedar tied to it. Essentially, the cedar represented the spirit and is located at the center, while horsehair tied at the top refer-ences her dark hair—she was a Kiowa woman. We then painted the tree with colors and just left it. We walked away from it on top of this hill. To me, it is interesting to look at this piece and think about the memorials and other historically oriented projects that I would work on later in the future. Perhaps Don Secondine helped me start out on that path.

## The *London Shape* & Philadelphia

I left Kansas because I had a scholarship to the Royal Col-lege of Art in London. I had a lot of trouble there with my work. London was not very hospitable to me in terms of found art materials, but it was a very engaging society on other levels. It was very multicultural, a bizarre kind of twist considering the colonial nature of the British Crown. You have all kinds of people coming to England, and I met those people. I traveled throughout Europe as well, but I spent a lot of my time just hanging out in Piccadilly Circus, the Times Square of England. While I was at the Royal College I made a series of work with imagery titled *London Shape* (Fig. 15). Each shape was constructed with pieces of colored illustration board. I could not do the trash art in

England (that I had done in Kansas) because it was not really feasible. So I went back and re-examined the print-making I had done, as well as earlier paintings. But, ultimately, I found *London Shape* to be kind of a dead end—it related to itself too much. I think art is bad when it relates only to itself. You have to go beyond your own practice, your own aesthetic, and engage the world.

As I traveled to see the Matisse chapel in Vence, the Vatican in Rome, the Van Gogh Museum in Amsterdam, and all around Europe, my interest in experiencing other cultural entities, such as people and places, deepened. Paradoxically, I found myself looking inward and experiencing the proverbial cultural cliché that travelers feel when they are away from home too long. That is, I wanted to go back home and learn more about the Cheyenne world. So I left England and came back to Oklahoma and lived with my Cheyenne grandmother, Lightning Woman. My grandmother had done a lot of beadwork, as had her own mother, Howling Crane. From their inspiration, I took a pattern of geometric mountain forms that Howling Crane had beaded into a woman's moccasin and made a print of the design (Fig. 16).

I then went to Philadelphia to the Tyler School of Art to finish my master of fine arts degree. My thesis was to take the modern art shape, or what I called the *London Shape,* and let it fight the beadwork, so to speak, when I painted both on the same paper. I also made a series of paintings to try to find out where I would start talking from, which allegiance I would choose and also have my art practices reflect. I made one painting that shows a Gourd Dance blanket that men wear in the Warrior Society, and it is red and blue with an appliqué pattern down the middle (Fig. 17). In the center you see the *London Shape,* which at this point is pretty much overwhelmed symbolically by the imagery from Oklahoma and the tribal life embedded therein. This then led me to make a series of red

paintings. I had quit working so formally in terms of geometric discourse and instead made a painting about my sisters and cousins titled *Win of Birds* (Fig. 18). In this piece, I took issue with the idea of how the West was won, which is often perceived as though it were a game. As such, my work became politicized, and I got a strong editorial going with this piece. I combined the idea of how the West was won with my name, so it reads: West of Birds, Win of Birds, Won of Birds, Lost of Birds, Heap of West, Heap of Win, Heap of Won, Heap of Lost. Also included on the piece is a close-up of a photograph of four young women, two sisters and two cousins, just laughing at a powwow. This photograph was kind of my locator. It indicates to the viewer that the West is not just a word or an idea—it is a big place, a powwow, kids laughing—and, most of all, that it is a very real, personal experience for me.

I also made a large painting in Philadelphia titled *Boil Broken Bones* (Fig. 19). It is a pretty funny painting. In referencing the concept of circularity during a time when there were a lot of misguided New Age ideas flying around, I was really forming a critique about mainstream society's idealization of man's so-called natural state. Obviously, this meant that Native Americans, and their ways of life, became unwitting stand-ins for an entire group's status quo. By making a perfect circle in the center of the piece, I am acknowledging the ideal nature, or goodness, inherent to circularity while at the same time juxtaposing it with cutout images of a mechanized machine, which, in fact, together make up the form of the circle. The red and blue colors bisecting the canvas refer to the warrior blanket mentioned above. The color photographs depict an Apache pop-up aluminum camper to point out that New Age ideas about naturalism are not only a façade, but that the appropriation of Native names or ideas to achieve it is counter-productive. In that way, this circle is not good because so much energy is expended to create it, and, in fact, energy is wasted. On the other hand, the title of the work, *Boil Broken Bones,* references a story about my grandmother, Lightning Woman, who boiled broken bones to release the marrow, resulting in a soup that people can eat. The ironic structure of the painting contrasts romantic, New Age ideology with the expediency that Lightning Woman foresaw in boiling broken bones and, in essence, not wasting a thing—what could be more natural?

Powwow Chair was important, too (Fig. 20). It is about a discussion I had with some people at a gallery opening who were asking me how you sit at a powwow. They said, "You must sit Indian style?" I said, "No, that is too hard on your back. You get a chair from Kmart and you put a blanket in it and you put your name on the back so no one steals it." So I wanted to make a piece to make that evident. I dug up earth in Oklahoma from my grandmother's house; then I took it to Philadelphia and created *Powwow Chair.* There is a card that reads: mixed media, powwow chair, Oklahoma earth, Pendleton blanket. Of course, everyone has access to these things that make up *Powwow Chair*—it is not a new thing. However, on the East Coast these objects were viewed as novelties even though I was presenting life as it really was. No one is sitting in it, but if you go to dances you know what it is.

In Philadelphia, there were very few Native people. It was kind of a strange community, a hard place to be a Native person. You would get stopped and asked weird questions. It was almost like you were a lizard running around town, like we were reptiles that were out of place. However, in our ceremonies they have lizard dancers, and I always wanted to become one. So "lizard" was a very important word to me nonetheless. When I graduated, my master of fine arts thesis show was titled *Lizards.* I made *Fort Marion Lizards* to honor my great-great-grandfather Many Magpies and all the chiefs and other Cheyenne and Arapaho prisoners of war who were held captive at Fort

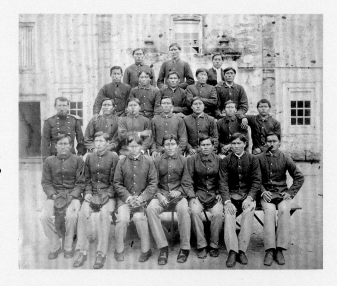

Fig. 6
*21 Indian Prisoners at Fort Marion with Captain Richard Pratt,* c. 1870

Marion, Florida, in the 1870s (Fig. 21). Years later someone sent me a copy of an article that had been previously printed in the Fort Marion newspaper. The author had reported that the Cheyenne prisoners were sunning themselves on the beach like lizards. Surprisingly, the person who sent the article to me told me that it was really great that I had gone back and made a piece about the article—but I had never read it before. My belief is that something was leading me to make *Fort Marion Lizards.* The four principal chiefs imprisoned were Minimic, Heap of Birds (Many Magpies), Eagle's Head, and Grey Beard (Fig. 6). I always try to honor them as I work. In fact, much of the content of *Wheel* is informed by these Cheyenne leaders, their experiences, and the events that shaped their lives.

30

## Oklahoma, Cleveland, Australia, Africa

Back to Oklahoma, back to the red earth, it taught me a lot. I made my first painting there about the land. It was not an easy homecoming for me after living on the East Coast while in graduate school. I came home to my Arapaho great-grandmother Nancy North's house, which had no water, no electricity, and no road. I lived there for twelve years on top of a canyon. That red rock canyon will always remain very important to me as a touchstone in my life. But it was hard to fit in. It certainly became a very strong home, but it took a lot of sweat equity to get to that point. The first painting I made is titled *Neuf Series #1* and has to do with the land, the breakup of the red rock (Fig. 22). It is not really a landscape painting, but it has something to do with it. The title is significant because "neuf" is a Cheyenne word meaning the number four, or to do something four times.

I also made a billboard in Oklahoma City. I do not do a lot of work in Oklahoma because of the political climate, but I have done a few things. This billboard—ƨᴙƎᴎOOƧ RUN OVER INDIAN NATIONS APARTHEID OKLAHOMA—was done to protest the one-hundredth-year anniversary of the Oklahoma Land Rush (Fig. 28). The billboard wound up causing a very important grassroots movement in the Native community. We made t-shirts, and there was a protest march to the Oklahoma State Capitol that had not been initially planned until after the billboard came to exist.

I have also caused a lot of trouble in Cleveland, Ohio. I designed a billboard titled *American Leagues* about the local baseball team, the Cleveland Indians, and it reads SMILE FOR RACISM (Fig. 32). When the team's supporters discuss the mascot, "Chief Wahoo," they say that it is honoring Native people, so I viewed it as a gift but took it upon myself to alter it. If someone gives something to you as a gift you can alter it or do whatever you want with it. Some people reacted unfavorably to the billboard and cited copyright infringement, indicating that it was destroying their mascot. The artwork was censored, but in the end, it got installed anyway. We made three or four billboards with the same message. The billboard became important to the Indian movement because it spurred discussions about mascot sensitivity and instigated great media exposure. It became a pretty important action in Cleveland.

I have also been working in Australia. First, I went out to the bush. I always do this as my method of operation in countries that I work in, especially if there are indigenous roots. I was asked to go and live on a reservation in Uluru, near Ayers Rock. There are Aboriginal sites there for prayer and fasting. I lived there and dug gum-tree roots with elders out in the bush. They then made carvings using the gum-tree roots. It was a really good orientation, learning about Aboriginal culture and exchanging cultures with them. I went into the inner cities later as well. I befriended an artist in Bondai, near Sydney, who had made a dreaming painting of snakes. I collaborated with her and many other artists there to make the *16 Songs* project, which later toured America. One example of the Aboriginal artists' work is by a man named Gordon Hookey, titled *New Growth* (Fig. 7). I gave those artists my work, honestly, as a gift, and they gave me theirs in response to the sixteen words or phrases associated with the project.[1]

One of the most profound experiences on my trip to Australia was going to the Great Barrier Reef. I have swum in many tropical reefs, from Belize to St. Croix to Samoa to Bali—all these islands and locations—but the Great Barrier Reef is the healthiest wilderness that I have found. I really enjoy the movement of the coral and the fish, and the colors are spectacular. You are buoyant; you cannot sink, so you just float along. This experience in the water really informed my paintings, it gave them a big boost, and I continued those paintings that I call the *Neuf* paintings

Fig. 7
*New Growth,* 1995
Gordon Hookey
Acrylic on canvas, 24 × 30 in.

(Fig. 34). The implied movement of the shapes is much like my dogs as they run when I am hunting in the red rock canyon, the clouds as they gather in the valley heading south to the Canadian River, or the fish that I see off Bali as I am snorkeling. Those positive experiences are depicted in a symbolic way by my shapes moving across the picture plane. I do not start the paintings with any drawings. I start with a blank canvas and paint the shapes one at a time until they are layered on top of one another. In the end, I may wind up covering up half my painting, which is a very frustrating experience, but I think it turns out to be a good thing. It is kind of a truce that you make with the painting. I stop when it is still a little bit out of control. I never really control it; I cannot control it; I just stop at one point and we call a truce. That is where the power lies. You do not want to break the spirit of the painting. You want the painting to have its own way about it.

I am also working on prints with Michael McCabe, a wonderful Native printer in Santa Fe. The prints consist of three-word phrases such as "that green money" or "you may enter" (Fig. 35). To give it context, I was lecturing at the National Gallery of Zimbabwe, where I was very popular at the Hilton Hotel because I had U.S. dollars. They called it "that green money." When you leave a tip at a restaurant, you might leave them the equivalent of six hundred "Zim" dollars with one U.S. dollar. "That green money" was kind of an entrée to many things in that country. Even though I am not necessarily a proponent of the United States, it was very powerful to have that money sometimes.

To make the prints, I use a paintbrush to apply a clear resist on Plexiglas while writing backward to make the words, or text. Then we run a roller saturated with ink on it—black, green, blue, any color we choose. Essentially, you get the ghosting effect of the words from the resist applied to the Plexiglas—how it pulls onto the paper as well as how it pulls the ink off the roller. The end product is very much happenstance; the paper is white, so what you are seeing are the letters becoming almost like clouds or smoke. I really enjoy the softness of the text. Most of my text is fairly solid in my public art, but I have been doing a lot of new monotypes that are softer, more ghostlike.

While I was in South Africa, I got to know a public art cooperative called Public Eye. They did a wonderful project that I would like to talk about briefly. It shows how one can do public art without a huge commission. You do not need a letter of intent or a permit if you want to do something, do it today or do it tonight. There is a heritage day in South Africa that celebrates South Africa's white heritage. There is a statue of P. W. Botha, president of South Africa during the apartheid era, and on the bottom of the statue it says, "Farmer, warrior, statesman" (Fig. 8). It is a typical heroic white man statue, not unlike the ones in the park across the street from the Denver Art Museum. Botha was there on his horse as the conquering statesman of South Africa. In the middle of the night, Public Eye went out and dressed him up as a Khoisan warrior. The Khoisan people have a puberty ceremony where they send their young men out to find their totem, or their way. So Public Eye dressed Botha up as a Khoisan warrior adolescent with a cloak and headdress, and they even gave him an Afro nose and painted him with ochre. Then they took photographs. The authorities rushed out and washed the statue off and took the cloak and headdress away, but before that there was already a picture sent to me in Oklahoma from South Africa. The art existed for a few hours, and now the image exists forever. I would encourage everyone to do some nonsanctioned public art.

## Ocmulgee and the Trail of Tears

I want to talk now about a project I did in the spring of 2005 when I was a visiting artist at the Atlanta College of Art. The project was about the prehistoric Ocmulgee pyramids located in Macon, Georgia. I found that people in Georgia were very naïve about the pyramids. No one knew

Fig. 8    *P.T.O. (Please Turn Over),* 2000
Beezy Bailey; A Public Eye Project
Art intervention

where or what they were. This shocked me so I felt compelled to research it myself. It was wonderful to see the accomplishments of the ancestral tribal nations in Georgia. At the site, there were two pyramids, a large one and a small one, that reveal complex knowledge systems in the areas of science and astronomy on a comparable astral and cultural significance to those structures located in Egypt, Stonehenge, and Mexico. In one component of the Ocmulgee project, I had students working with me in the gallery to re-create the Ocmulgee pyramids in wood with rag paper applied over them (Fig. 36). I had researched the ceramic artifact designs from the Ocmulgee village and drew these designs on the pyramids with the help of students. Ocmulgee is a very large, wonderful site that is attuned to what

Fig. 9    Big Horn Medicine Wheel, Wyoming

is happening above us as are most Native American–made monuments. With the Ocmulgee project, my work sought to bring the history of Native American traditions, tribal accomplishments, and the art of the Muscogee (Creek) Nation to contemporary citizens of Georgia.

The second component of the Ocmulgee project consisted of a series of forty-eight metal sign panels to commemorate the forcible removal of Native tribes from their traditional homelands in Georgia to the western United States in what is known as the Trail of Tears (Fig. 37). The red text messages are created in a four-part series and duplicated in twelve sets. These panels were attached to eight-foot-tall street sign posts and installed throughout the Peachtree area and Woodruff Arts Center of downtown Atlanta. So not only was there work in the gallery, but we also had work out on Peachtree Street. The students helped

me put the signs up. The four panels read: DO YOU CHOOSE TO WALK, WERE YOU FORCED TO WALK, TRAIL OF TEARS 1836, WALK TO OKLAHOMA. The piece was about modern-day pedestrian habits and was a comment about people walking to work or power walking for exercise. What my signs were trying to say is, "when you are power walking in Atlanta, maybe you can keep on going to Oklahoma." The piece was talking to people all along the street and, hopefully, educated the pedestrians of Atlanta to remember the suffering of tribal peoples by the hands of U.S. governmental removal policies via forced walks that began in 1836. Later, Georgia College and State University in Milledgeville, Georgia, collected four of the signs, and installed them permanently on campus.

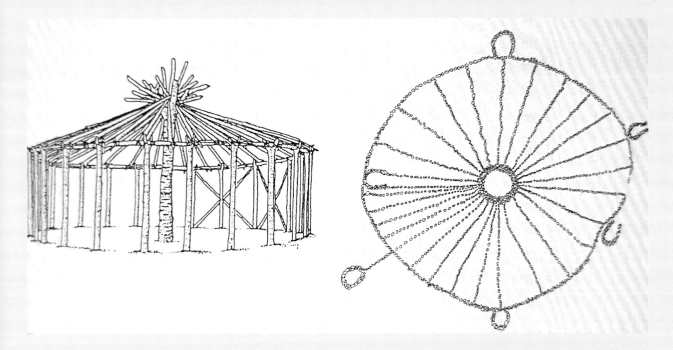

Fig. 10    Sun Dance Lodge and Medicine Wheel

## Wheel

I did research for a year or two before I launched into *Wheel*. At each juncture, I was changing, adapting to the ideas and contemplating the history. Primarily, you can see the formation of my project because it stems from working with the medicine wheel at Big Horn, Wyoming (Fig. 9). If one were to take this medicine wheel formation, you might get a very close approximation of the top view of rafters of the earth renewal lodge (Fig. 10). This circular formation can be found from Alberta all the way down to Oklahoma with tribal groups located on the east face of the Rockies, because we share similar religious practices and belief systems. I visited the Big Horn Medicine Wheel twice with my sons and made my own offerings there. In fact, the Cheyennes have been going there for the same reason for hundreds of years.

I positioned *Wheel*'s individual trees in the exact position of the astral notations also made at Big Horn, which variously reference Rigel rising, Sirius rising, the solstice sunrise, and so on. All those key solar and stellar positions were outlined by the ancient ones using stone cairns that form a wheel at Big Horn. I acknowledged these same positions through the placement of the trees in the sculpture at the Denver Art Museum. In addition, I thought very hard about the formation of *Wheel* itself, because many of the original ceremonial earth renewal lodges have twelve locators, and we still have our ceremonial circle that is built every year in the summer that way. In that sense, I think it is very important for Native artists to realize that when one is making, or creating, modern art, it is essential, especially for me, to make sure it does not subvert religious aspects of sacred tribal knowledge. To me, *Wheel* represents a personal, creative expression outside of the religious realm; I felt strongly enough about this that I omitted two of the standing trees in favor of a total of ten. In that sense, *Wheel* is rendered dysfunctional as a ceremonial site; it is not a bona fide Cheyenne ceremonial apparatus because certain elements are inaccessible. On the other hand, I am certainly committed to the practice of my own religion, and since we have a process of creating our apparatus in a sanctioned way, I will continue to do so. The *Wheel* sculpture is just a piece of art.

The astral observations that were made by the tribes that created the Big Horn Medicine Wheel are not unique. This solar system is shared by all on a global basis; however, indigenous tribes interpret it in different ways. I travel, and I am kind of a student of renewal sites, so I have been to Peru, Ireland, and other places that contain these sites, such as the numerous pyramids around Mexico. One of the unifying observations is that indigenous people usually identify the movements of the sun, whether it is the winter or summer solstice or the spring equinox. Indigenous tribes have always observed these occasions with the movement of the planets and solar system to give value to their lives—and their art practices reflect this as well. I see these astral observations as a unifying feature; all cultures use this in their artwork. For example, the wheel at Big Horn can be about the life of a Cheyenne or Arapaho person, but on another level, the astral orientations can apply to lifeways in Zimbabwe or Indonesia as well. Wherever cultures are close to the Earth, they will make these astronomical markers.

The trees in *Wheel* are very complex. A lot of the drawings and imagery that I reference find specificity with the events surrounding Fort Marion. My family was heavily impacted by Fort Marion because my great-great-grandfather Chief Many Magpies was imprisoned there with other members of the tribe. After the key Cheyenne leaders were released, life as they knew it beforehand had changed because of the transition to the reservation period and subsequent U.S. policies impacting Indian life on the social, political, religious, and economic levels. My name HOCK E AYE VI means "Little Chief," and the first man to have that name was also at Fort Marion (he was Many Magpies's nephew). So I feel connected in a very real way to the prisoners who endured hardships throughout all that history as if it comes directly down to me in the present day. Therefore, in some ways, I feel like I inherited some ownership of the artwork that was done in prison by my relatives, which is why I bring it back out, because they were the best people to observe that transition—that crushing colonial power in America on the Cheyenne

nation. They manifested it in their artwork. They would draw the schoolteacher, for example, in their own vision, and I took that drawing and subverted it to show the diminishing power of the white schoolteacher by replacing her with a traditional petroglyph of a woman that came out of the rock art of Colorado—I let that female image grow bigger and the white schoolteacher grow smaller (Fig. 39). I would hope that today we are not still indoctrinating people of color all the time into the colonial culture—that we are letting them manifest their own vision. So I used those images from Fort Marion, from my family. And the magpie that appears on the tenth tree is actually from a drawing that was done in prison as well. On that tree, my name, "Heap of Birds," which translates to "Many Magpies," is symbolically represented by the three magpies flying upward (Fig. 40).

Going back to my father and his forefathers, the reservation era was very difficult for many Indian people at the turn of the century. That lineage from the Fort Marion prisoners causes me to think of my own father; his name is Many Magpies. My father's life path was defined by living in a camping tent as a young boy, going to boarding school, graduating from high school, and becoming a parent and a very diligent factory worker at an aircraft plant for twenty-eight years. He raised me up with five other siblings, and I contrast that with my own life as I have been a professor at Yale University and the University of Oklahoma. I see my father's life choices as being empowered by Cheyenne traditional ways of life because of the way he grew up. I think of myself and how I came back to the reservation as well, how after graduate school I became an instructor of the ceremonies, so I have that dual education. In mentioning all this personal history about my father and myself, I am relating it to the final tree because it has all the acronyms of advanced educational degrees listed (Fig. 11). Alongside the degrees are symbolic references to the ancient warrior

36

Fig. 11    *Wheel, Tree 10,* 2005
Edgar Heap of Birds
Porcelain on steel, 144 × 24 × 24 in.

twins, Monster Slayer and Born for Water, who are very important heroes to tribal groups in the Southwest. The tree is relating the fact that for Native men and women today, education is the new battle we are engaged in, whereas in the past, the battle had been with the U.S. Cavalry or other entities. Finally, with the form of the wheel—the ceremonial circle—you have that education where you can become empowered by your own traditions.

The text on the wall, NAH-KEV-HO-EYEA-ZIM, comes from my grandmother, Lightning Woman, also known as Alice Heap of Birds (Fig. 5). In the 1980s, when she was still alive, I asked her about a phrase for how the Cheyenne would talk about returning home—turning back around to where we come from. She said, "nah-kev-ho-eyea-zim," and I thought that was a fitting emblem for the *Wheel* project. The phrase finds context here in Denver because from the east face of the Rocky Mountains to the Platte River to the Arkansas River and to Kansas itself, that was the land granted to us in the Treaty of Fort Laramie. I wanted to make that clear in terms of the big text on the wall—that this place was our homeland in the 1870s and before. So when *Wheel* comes back as it has done here in Denver, Colorado, that means we are home again as well.

37

## Note

1. The sixteen words or phrases are: Sky, Earth, Offering, Patience, Trees, Strength, Sing, New Growth, Green, Four, Awareness, Resistance, Solstice, For Everyone, Dance, Water.

Selected Works
of
HOCK E AYE VI
Edgar Heap of Birds

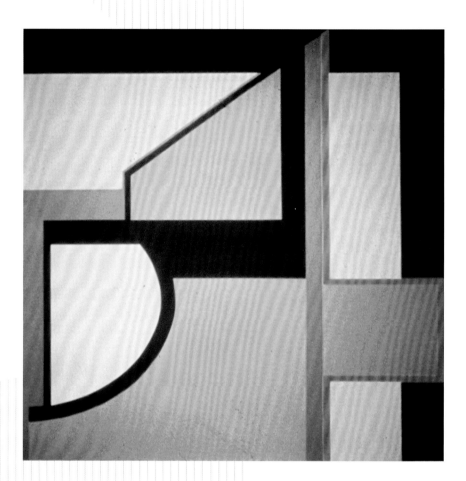

Fig. 12    *Untitled,* 1974
           **Edgar Heap of Birds**
           Acrylic on canvas, 6 × 6 ft.

Fig. 13    *Construction,* 1976
           Edgar Heap of Birds
           Mixed media installation, 8 × 12 ft.

Fig. 14     *Kiowa Memorial,* 1976
Edgar Heap of Birds, Don Secondine
Horse hair, acrylic paint, cedar branches, and single tree, 25 ft.

Fig. 15
*London Shape,* 1977
Edgar Heap of Birds
Acrylic paint on illustration board,
12 × 16 ft.

42

Fig. 16
*Howling Crane,* 1977
Edgar Heap of Birds
Serigraph, 24 × 36 in.

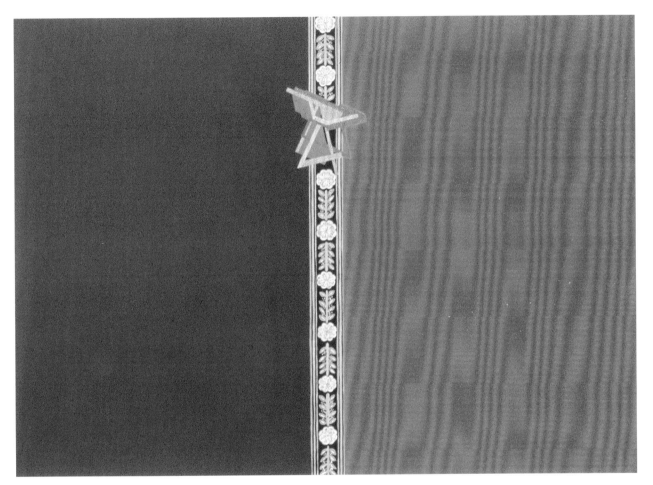

Fig. 17    *Red Dirt Contrast*, 1978
Edgar Heap of Birds
Tempera on paper, 36 × 49 in.

Fig. 18    *Win of Birds,* 1978
Edgar Heap of Birds
Mixed media on paper, 24 × 36 in.

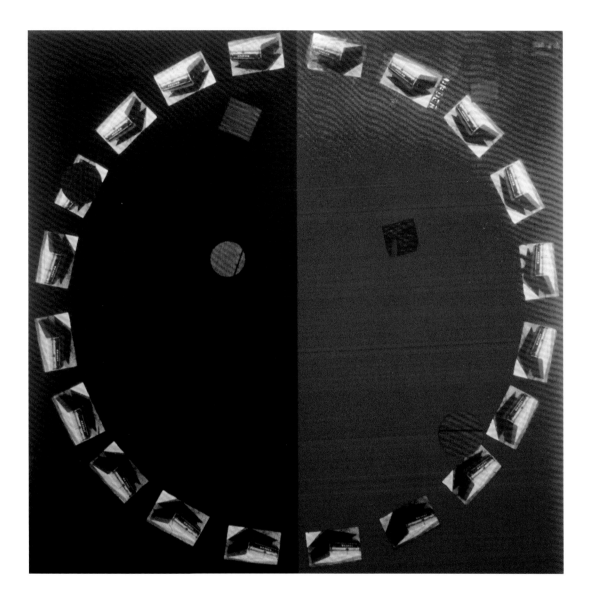

Fig. 19    *Boil Broken Bones,* 1979
Edgar Heap of Birds
Acrylic paint and photographs on canvas, 8 × 8 ft.

Fig. 20    *Powwow Chair,* 1979
           Edgar Heap of Birds
           Aluminum lawn chair, Pendleton blanket,
           and Oklahoma earth, 48 × 48 in.

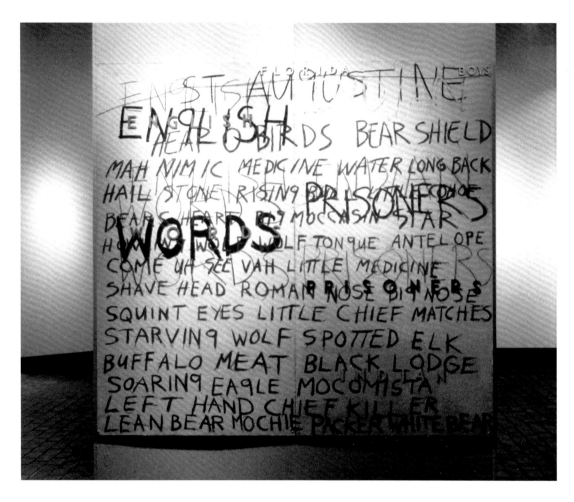

Fig. 21    *Fort Marion Lizards,* 1979
Edgar Heap of Birds
Acrylic on wall board, 8 × 8 ft.

48

Fig. 22     *Neuf Series #1,* 1981
Edgar Heap of Birds
Acrylic on canvas board, 8 × 10 in.

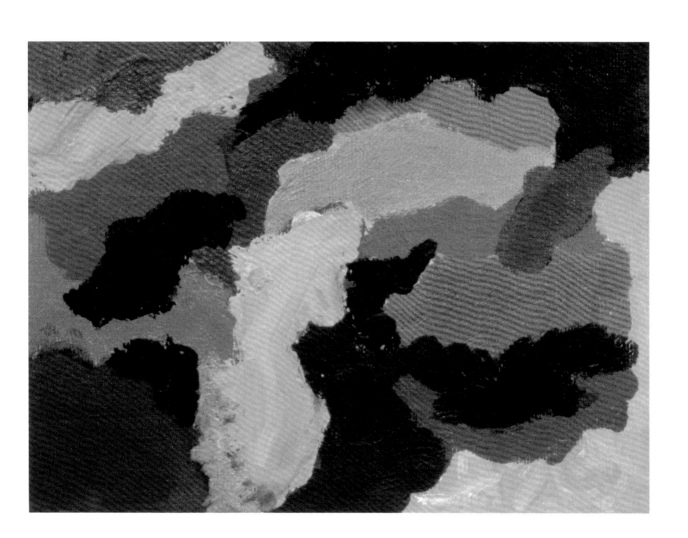

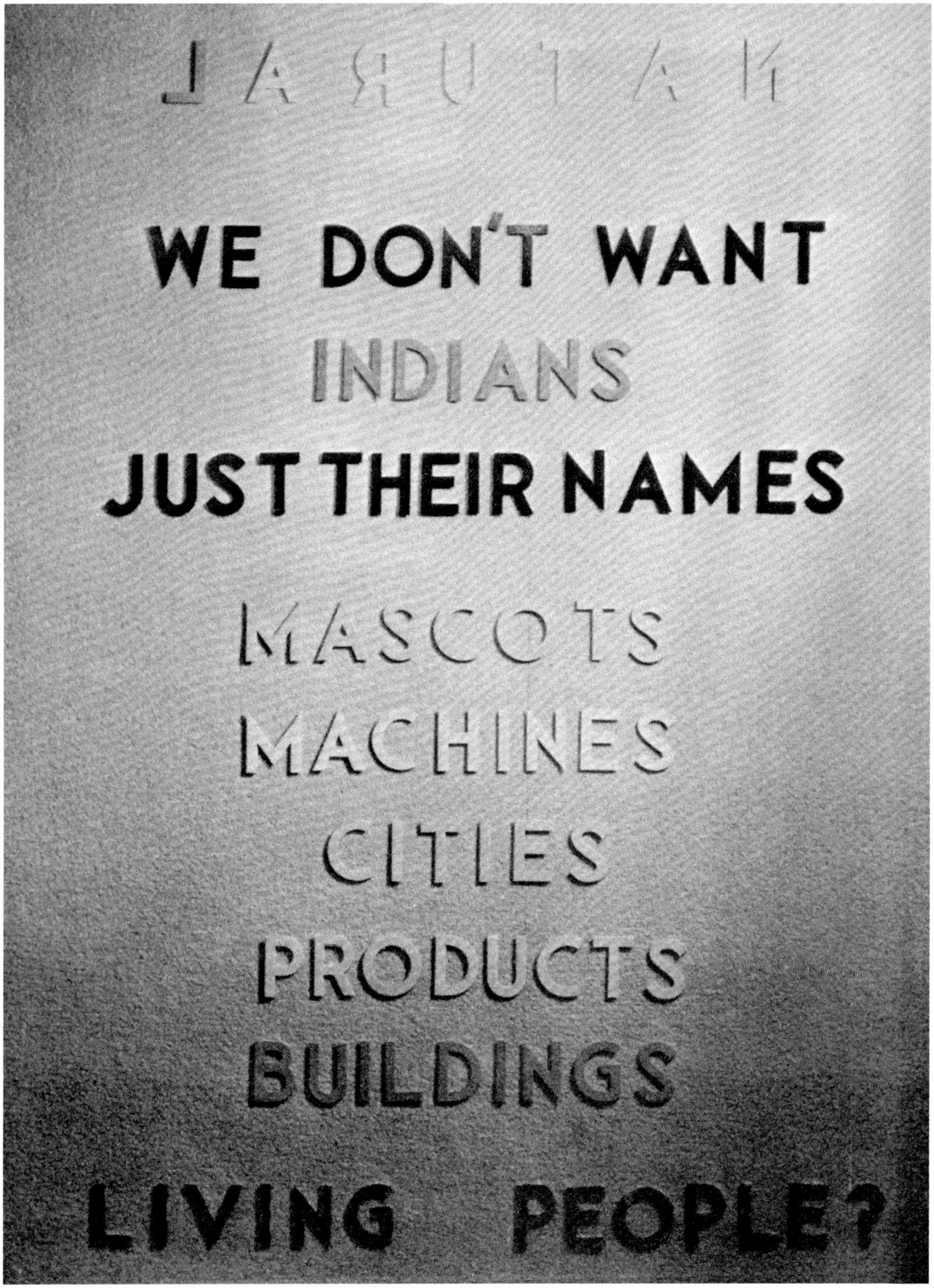

Fig. 23    *Don't Want Indians,* 1982
Edgar Heap of Birds
Die-cut letters on wall, 8 × 5 ft.

Fig. 24    *In Our Language,* 1982
         Edgar Heap of Birds
         Computer light billboard, 20 × 40 ft.

Fig. 25     *Death from the Top,* 1983
            Edgar Heap of Birds
            Painted die-cut letters on wall, 8 × 20 ft.

Fig. 26    *South African Homelands,* 1986
           Edgar Heap of Birds
           Painted stencil text mural on wall, 8 × 20 ft.

Fig. 27
*Telling Many Magpies, Telling
Black Wolf, Telling Hachivi,* 1989
Edgar Heap of Birds
Serigraph, 62 × 42 in.

Fig. 28
*Apartheid Oklahoma,* 1989
Edgar Heap of Birds
Billboard, ink on paper, 5 × 9 ft.

Fig. 29      *Mission Gifts,* 1990
             Edgar Heap of Birds
             Paper bus banner, 3 × 9 ft.

Fig. 30    *Building Minnesota,* 1990
Edgar Heap of Birds
Screen printing on metal panels, 18 × 36 in. each
400-ft. outdoor installation

Fig. 31     *Learn a War Cry,* 1994
            Edgar Heap of Birds, Fiona Foley
            Mylar text on wall, 8 × 7 ft.

Fig. 32    *American Leagues,* 1996
            Edgar Heap of Birds
            Commercial billboard, 6 × 12 ft.

THUS WAS GOD CRUSHING
HIS PROUD ENEMIES
BURNING THEM UP IN FIRE
DUNGING THE GROUND
WITH THEIR FLESH
IT IS MARVELLOUS IN
OUR EYES

MANY WERE BURNED
MEN WOMEN AND CHILDREN
OTHERS WERE FORCED OUT
WHICH OUR SOLDIERS
RECEIVED AND ENTERTAINED
WITH THE POINT OF THE SWORD

Fig. 33    *Dunging the Ground,* 1996
         Edgar Heap of Birds
         Mylar text on steel panels, 42 × 60 in. each

Fig. 34  *Neuf Series,* 1997
Edgar Heap of Birds
Acrylic on canvas, 89 × 105 in.

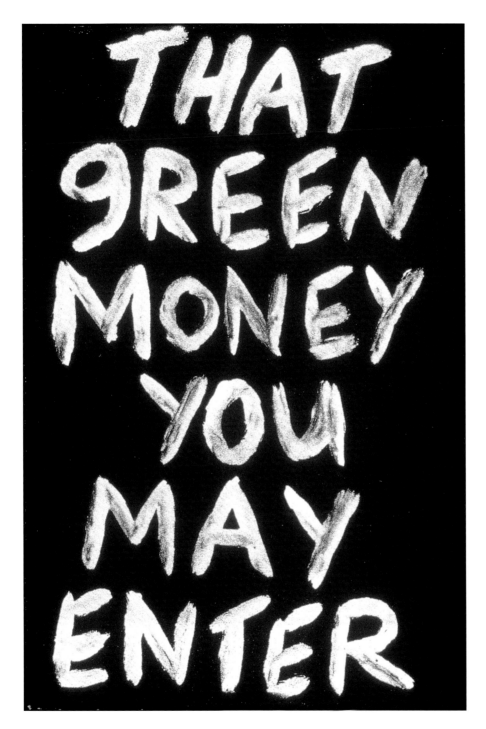

Fig. 35    *You May Enter*, 2004
           Edgar Heap of Birds
           Monoprint, 22 × 15 in.

Fig. 36    Ocmulgee exhibition
Atlanta College of Art
March 10–April 24, 2005

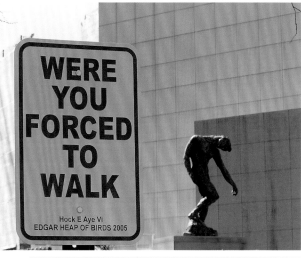

Fig. 37    *Ocmulgee,* 2005
Edgar Heap of Birds
Mylar on metal sign panels, 18 × 12 in. each

Fig. 38        *Wheel,* 2005
              Edgar Heap of Birds
              Porcelain on steel, diam. 50 ft.

Fig. 39        *Wheel, Tree 8,* 2005
              Edgar Heap of Birds
              Porcelain on steel, 144 × 24 × 24 in.

Fig. 40        *Wheel, Tree 10,* 2005
              Edgar Heap of Birds
              Porcelain on steel, 144 × 24 × 24 in.

Edgar Heap of Birds's *Wheel,* which was dedicated on June 21, 2005, marked a major moment in the history of Native American art and in the life of the Denver Art Museum, long noted for the quality of its Indian art collection, which includes numerous twentieth-century paintings and sculptures as well as historic objects. *Wheel* (see Fig. 38) is a circular installation, fifty feet in diameter, of ten bright red vertical forms, each twelve feet tall, that branch into a "Y" shape at the top. These porcelain-enameled "trees," as the artist calls them, are screenprinted with images and texts that relate to Native history in what is now the state of Colorado. Seemingly assertive and confident, the standing forms reference architecture, ancient monuments, and the human figure. More suggestive than descriptive, they function as storytellers and sentinels. Given the scale and the specificity of the site—next to an entrance of a major urban museum—*Wheel* was a significant project with a long gestation period. *Wheel* thus embodies the Denver Art Museum's commitment to contemporary art, just as it stands as the high-water mark of an accomplished artist at midcareer. And although *Wheel* is Heap of Birds's first large-scale permanent installation, it was preceded by a number of important public art projects that investigate history and give form to traumatic memory, often through symbolic inversion. In this essay I want to contextualize *Wheel* by reviewing, albeit briefly, Heap of Birds's development, focusing primarily on public art. In the conclusion I will mention very briefly the work of some other artists to underscore the larger family of objects and aesthetic strategies to which *Wheel* belongs.[1]

Heap of Birds, who is deeply committed to Cheyenne-Arapaho ceremonial life in Oklahoma, has established an international reputation for his art, which includes earth-awareness abstractions called *Neuf* paintings and painterly word drawings that he calls "wall lyrics." He has also produced printed messages and signs for public art

The Prehistory of *Wheel*
Symbolic Inversions and
Traumatic Memory in the Art
of Edgar Heap of Birds
*by W. Jackson Rushing III*

*Wheel* dedication, June 21, 2005

commissions. Typically, the wall lyrics are gestural, personal, and richly ambiguous—open to multiple readings—while the prints and public signs are written in the visual form and rhetoric of corporate and governmental power. That is, they *look* objective and authoritative (like historical markers and highway signs), while they both claim and subvert institutional language.

But why work with words instead of images? The most obvious answer is that Heap of Birds participates in a widespread postmodern/conceptual art impulse that emerged in the early 1980s and investigates the complex relationship between language, "reality," and power.[2] Indeed, his inclusion in several important group exhibitions in the 1980s testifies to the fact that his early language pieces helped define their moment in time.

For example, in 1985 he exhibited *Death from the Top* (1983; Fig. 25), which features three columns of words made with painted die-cut letters on an eight by twenty-foot section of wall. Lacking all pretensions to "art," especially color and facture, it is the example par excellence of what Hal Foster called the anti-aesthetic in contemporary art.[3] Some of the phrases are written backward, which is a symbolic inversion, or Heap of Birds's cue for the audience to read backward, that is, to think historically. All of the phrases are written in capital letters, and they constitute a soundless précis of murderous rage and lamentation. He was and is sickened by the memory of Cheyenne people murdered and then mutilated along the Washita River by Colonel George Custer's Seventh Cavalry in 1868. But he refused to make what he called "syrupy narrative paintings" about victimization. Lamenting mainstream culture's amnesia about colonial violence, he chose instead to make what he calls "notations," such as

FORGET/FORGOT, SLEEPING/CHILDREN, RUNNING/CHILDREN, KILL/MY PEOPLE, DESTROY/EARTH.

Heap of Birds's embrace of words and language in the late 1970s–early 1980s also reflects his keen awareness of what Jacques Derrida called the anthropological battle that commences when colonizers superimpose their imported language(s) on Native names and speech.[4] And yet, let's be candid: Native peoples in the Americas didn't need poststructural theory to know that since 1492 language has been a tool of ideology formation and, therefore, violence against indigenous cultures. For example, *Fort Marion Lizards* (1979; Fig. 21) lists the names of the Cheyenne and Arapaho prisoners of war, including Heap of Birds's relatives, who were incarcerated at Fort Marion, Florida, in 1875–78. Many of these prisoners were artists who made ledger book drawings, which are now esteemed as cultural art(ifacts) that document armed conflict, deracination, and the psychic dislocations of the early reservation period. Heap of Birds has long identified with these warrior-artists, and *Fort Marion Lizards* is a key early work in terms of establishing the primacy of words in his artistic arsenal. These lizards or captives, he stated in 1981, "were not only imprisoned by [the] walls of the stockade; they were in a more emphatic sense captives of the English language that was used to ineptly alter their names."[5] In this context, the work declares ENGLISH WORDS/PRISONERS INDIAN, and it lists his family name, which the U.S. military changed at that time from Hachivi (Many Magpies) to Heap O' Birds and then to Heap of Birds.[6]

Heap of Birds is highly attuned to the effects that different formats and mediums can offer him when working with words and how recasting a work with a shift in title presents possibilities for new content. *Don't Want*

*Indians* (1982; Fig. 23) belongs to a group of early word works (also including *Death from the Top*), which are written with painted die-cut letters and whose formal austerity belies the anguish and complexity of their encrypted messages. The text is bracketed at the top by NATURAL (spelled backward) and at the bottom by LIVING PEOPLE? In between, a disembodied but apparently official voice announces,

> WE DON'T WANT INDIANS / JUST THEIR NAMES / MASCOTS / MACHINES / CITIES / PRODUCTS / BUILDINGS

The piece resembles the wall labels from the 1940s that *still* accompanied antiquated installations of Native material culture at George Heye's Museum of the American Indian in upper Manhattan in 1982. Heap of Birds substantially altered the mood and meaning of *Don't Want Indians* when he reworked and retitled it *Telling Many Magpies, Telling Black Wolf, Telling Hachivi* (1989; Fig. 27). In this latter version the words fight for recognition amid a fluttering field of black shapes that refers both to magpies and the organic pulse of his landscape abstractions. Fully exploiting the graphic potential of words and shapes struggling for coexistence on the surface, Heap of Birds finds a bold, dark beauty absent in the nondescript *Don't Want Indians*. The title, too, both clarifies and mystifies by foregrounding the names of his ancestors: Black Wolf was a headsman of the Cheyenne Elk Clan, a son of Chief Heap of Birds (a Fort Marion prisoner), and the artist's great grandfather.[7] The artist is himself a headsman in the Cheyenne Elk Clan, and he may be establishing his right to "tell" their story, to speak on their behalf. Alternatively, perhaps he is telling *them* that although the struggle continues more than a hundred years later, he is, in his own words, still "on the edge of the battle to inform and re-educate the white man about his Native host."[8]

The year 1982 also marked his first major public art commission, a computer billboard project in Times Square. His electronic sign, titled *In Our Language* (Fig. 24), is a pendant to *Don't Want Indians,* because it, too, turned an indigenous eye on mainstream culture, flashing nine phrases across the screen:

> IN OUR LANGUAGE / TSISTSISTAS "CHEYENNE" / SPEAK OF VEHOE /
>    TSISTSISTAS SAID VEHOE WRAPPED UP / TSISTSISTAS SAID VEHOE FENCED IN / TSISTSISTAS SAID VEHOE CATCH YOU / TSISTSISTAS SAID VEHOE TRAP YOU / TSISTSISTAS SAID VEHOE SPIDER / TSISTSISTAS SAID VEHOE WHITE MAN.

Like many of the interventions gathered under the Conceptual art umbrella, *In Our Language* engaged in what came to be known as "identity politics." Similarly, it was site-specific, ephemeral, and reliant on mass-media technology. Working with metaphoric mystery and the untranslatable (in the purest sense, at least), the piece also confounded the binary opposition of margin and center by delivering a radical critique from the "margin" in the heart of the "center." That is, recalling the spider webs that entangled him as he hunted down in the canyon on the Cheyenne rez, Heap of Birds took his message to the streets of Manhattan (as did Jean-Michel Basquiat, with his SAMO writing, 1977–79), *advertising* the undeniable fact that Vehoe / Spider / White Man has tricked, caught, wrapped up, and fenced in Heap of Birds's Cheyenne people.[9]

In 1990 Heap of Birds again intervened in public space with *Mission Gifts* (Fig. 29), a billboard project produced in conjunction with the San Jose Museum of Art. In an effort to *make places specific,* he always researches the history of Native-white relations relative to the placement of the work, rather than coming into a city and creating public art about himself or his tribe back home. Thus one of the signs in this series, which were placed on buses in the city's public transit system, denounced the legacy of Spanish mission "culture" in California:

SYPHILIS / SMALL POX / FORCED BAPTISMS /
MISSION GIFTS / ENDING NATIVE LIVES.

Clearly, in his public art he has been willing to incorporate the same information systems and formats used by promoters of consumer culture because he finds it "effective to challenge the white man" by means of the mass media. He reasons that "as in American business and culture, in order to survive in art one must communicate mass appeal."[10]

Another signage project, *Building Minnesota* (1990; Fig. 30), which was commissioned by the Walker Art Center in Minneapolis, consisted of forty signs bearing the names, in both Dakota and English, of Dakota prisoners of war executed by hanging in 1862 and 1865 under warrants signed by President Abraham Lincoln and later by President Andrew Johnson. Beneath each Dakota name are the words DEATH BY HANGING. The word HONOR, which appears at the top of each sign, functions as both imperative and descriptor. Comparing this project to Maya Lin's Vietnam Veterans Memorial, curator Joan Rothfuss observed that the installation impressed the local Native community, which responded by making numerous pilgrimages to the site of the installation along the banks of the Mississippi River near downtown Minneapolis.[11] By placing the signs next to an industrial and commercial district along the river, Heap of Birds intended not only to create signs of respect, but also to underscore the fact that "it was the potential disruption of American commerce that cost the Dakota people their lives."[12] In honoring the dead, Heap of Birds wants to replace racist and romantic images of Indians with what he has described as the "stunning reality" of the "true existence of Native Americans"—

awareness of which must, of necessity, precede any "truly sweeping social justice" for the host people.[13]

Some measure of justice, at least, is concentrated in Heap of Birds's new visual histories of past events. When the Wadsworth Atheneum commissioned a public art piece, his research led him to the massacre of seven hundred Pequot men, women, and children near Mystic, Connecticut, in 1637. Soldiers from the Connecticut and Massachusetts Bay colonies torched the Pequot fort and murdered many of the inhabitants as they tried to escape; those few that survived were enslaved by the colonists and rival tribes. According to curator Andrea Miller-Keller, "the Puritans justified their attack on Fort Mystic as divinely ordained." The Puritans, she writes, "described themselves as God's children in the wilderness, wholly righteous, threatened by the Pequots who were agents of Satan testing their faith." However, she reports that new evidence strongly suggests that the slaughter was motivated "as much by economic ambition as by concerns for public safety."[14] Heap of Birds called attention to this seventeenth-century nation-building violence with *Dunging the Ground* (1996; Fig. 33), a pair of steel memorial signs silk-screened with text that he installed on the museum's front lawn. In his project statement, Heap of Birds noted that when the "American colony patriots" burned the Pequots to death, the "lowest ebb of the human spirit was personified by their wicked actions, dark words and the pride that followed."[15] He chose to let the dark pride speak for itself by printing appropriated text. The message on the left-hand sign was written in 1637 by Captain John Mason, commander of the Connecticut Colony Militia:

THIS WAS GOD CRUSHING / HIS PROUD
ENEMIES / BURNING THEM UP IN FIRE /
DUNGING THE GROUND / WITH THEIR FLESH /
IT IS MARVELOUS IN / OUR EYES!

Captain John Underhill, commander of the Massachusetts Bay Colony Militia, provided the other text (1637):

MANY WERE BURNED/MEN, WOMEN AND CHILDREN/OTHERS WERE FORCED OUT/ WHICH OUR SOLDIERS/RECEIVED AND ENTERTAINED/WITH THE POINT OF THE SWORD.

For the artist, "it is profoundly sorrowful" that such murderous violence is a "true legacy and foundation of the American nation."[16] And yet, there is seldom ever any public discourse in the United States about murder as a foundational quality of the nation, in spite of the fact that an invisible thread runs from Columbus's murder of Taino people in the Caribbean, to Fort Mystic, to the Washita River, to the massacre of miners by management in Ludlow, Colorado, in 1914, to the thousands of black lynchings in the post–Civil War South, to My Lai in Vietnam in 1968, and now to Afghanistan and Iraq. Unfortunately, this nightmare, like the "native burning screams"[17] at Fort Mystic, is real, the horrific twin of the American Dream. Amazingly, though, Heap of Birds still seeks to emphasize the good that is possible:

It is my hope that through the health of our mutual futures we can establish predominantly positive affinities of culture within this country. Respect shall be the mainstay of such human development; whereby God, through diverse belief systems, will only nurture life and not be asked to promote death.[18]

Although the strength of *Dunging the Ground* and related works is their engagement with local narratives, Heap of Birds has made the world his purview. For almost twenty years he has avoided the insularity and parochial limitations of some Native American contemporary art by producing art that links indigenous communities and issues around the globe and by collaborating with and promoting Aboriginal artists internationally. During the height of campus unrest in the United States over university investments in companies doing business in South Africa, he pointed out the failure of progressive politics to confront apartheid at home in the very first of his public signs, *South African Homelands* (1986; Fig. 26). Hand-painted by college students following his original design, it was installed outdoors at Cleveland State University in 1987. The text of the sign announced:

OH!/THOSE SOUTH AFRICAN/HOMELANDS/ YOU IMPOSE/U.S. INDIAN RESERVATIONS.

In his accompanying essay Heap of Birds stressed the obvious similarities between "homelands" and "reservations," writing that both South Africa and the United States "dominated their Native hosts by establishing reserves and relocating the indigenous peoples for the profits and pleasures of the dominant culture."[19] The "you" of "you impose U.S. Indian reservations" is nonspecific, but it does implicate the reader in the completion of the work. Its implicit challenge is this: Did being indignant about racism in apartheid South Africa absolve "you" from a commitment to social justice for those Native Americans whose "homelands" are often prisons of inequity?

And what of the legal sanctity of the reservations themselves? Another site-specific signage installation, *Apartheid Oklahoma* (1989; see Fig. 28), addressed this issue directly during the one-hundredth anniversary of the Oklahoma Land Rush, a time when the U.S. government allowed non-Native people to claim "unassigned" lands in Oklahoma Indian Territory. Two million acres that were ostensibly "reserved" for Native tribes were opened by federal mandate to white settlers, many of whom began their rush for land before the official starting time—thus the name "Sooners." In defiance of the centenary celebration, Native peoples of Oklahoma marched in protest through downtown Oklahoma City to the state capitol. In solidarity and with the support of the Indian Youth Project, Heap of Birds installed five signs downtown and in nearby Norman, where he teaches at the University of Oklahoma, which read,

SOONERS/RUN OVER/INDIAN NATIONS/ APARTHEID OKLAHOMA.

For Heap of Birds and his peers, the "picnics, parades, carnivals and playground programs" of Sooner Days are "exercises in racism and cover-ups of true . . . American history [that] must be answered." In a historically informed gesture of anticelebration, he "deployed" *Apartheid Oklahoma* in what he still refers to as "Oklahoma Indian Territory."[20]

In the summer of 1994, following his participation in earth renewal ceremonies in western Oklahoma, Heap of Birds traveled to Australia, where he spent time working with and mentoring his Aboriginal colleagues. They shared cultural information and colonial histories, and he initiated a collaborative project by introducing sixteen "songs" to the artists, who were encouraged to respond by singing their own version, so to speak, in visual art. The songs, which are words and phrases, refer to renewal through ceremony, and resistance through indigenous solidarity. They also embody his belief in the unifying quality of the natural world. The sixteen songs are as follows: SKY, EARTH, OFFERING, PATIENCE, TREES, STRENGTH, SING, NEW GROWTH, GREEN, FOUR, AWARENESS, RESISTANCE, SOLSTICE, FOR EVERYONE, DANCE, and WATER. The resulting work was organized by curator Diana Block into a group exhibition titled *16 Songs: Issues of Personal Assessment and Indigenous Renewal,* which traveled from 1995 to 2000. In collaboration with Heap of Birds, the Aboriginal artist Fiona Foley installed a language piece titled *Learn a War Cry* (1994; Fig. 31) at the Museum of Contemporary Art in Sydney, which featured a column of Aboriginal words

in dialogue with a column of Cheyenne words. According to Mohawk curator Lee-Ann Martin, *Learn a War Cry* engages "in a dialogue within the context of colonialism and commonwealth." She noted also "that the work addresses the universal conflicts and tensions within the histories of indigenous peoples worldwide."[21]

With these precedents in mind, let us turn again to *Wheel,* a sculptural installation attuned to the summer solstice sunrise that honors the sun's passage over the land. Dramatic and provocative, its shape (both round and vertical) has several important antecedents: the stele of ancient Mexico; the astral medicine wheels of the intermountain area of North America (such as the one near Big Horn, Wyoming); the circular kivas or sacred underground chambers of ancient and contemporary Puebloan peoples; and the Plains Indian earth renewal lodge. According to the artist, "the content within this solstice wheel will be the history and future of Colorado territory's past and present Native American population and their interaction with the politics of American life." In his original proposal for the commission, he wrote, "this modern day *Wheel* seeks to educate the diverse citizens and visitors of Colorado. An enlightenment can occur if a truthful view of the Native American experience of destruction, evolution and a rebuilding of cultural identity is realized."[22]

In its permanence and emphasis on sculptural form, *Wheel* marks a shift in Heap of Birds's practice, even as it continues his use of words and historical research. Familiar also is the commingling of ancient belief systems, awareness of colonial history, and hope for healing and renewal. Indeed, his rigorous scrutiny of history always serves a vision of the future notable for its generosity and its yearning for justice, respect, and peace for the Earth and *all* its peoples. And *Wheel* once again makes tangible his belief that art is like an arrow point or "sharp rock" that both preserves and defends.

In closing I want to mention, very briefly, four works of art to which *Wheel* can be favorably compared. The first of these is Maya Lin's Vietnam Veterans Memorial, dedicated in 1982, the year in which Heap of Birds installed *In Our Language* in Times Square. A sober, site-specific sculpture, the memorial refers to both ancient and contemporary earthworks, as it allows names to honor the dead without glorifying the conflict in which they died. Second, I think of the "Crucifixion of Culture Series" (1995), a powerful suite of copper-plate etchings by the Laguna Pueblo artist Floyd Solomon, which documents the horrific colonial violence inflicted on Pueblo peoples in the seventeenth century by such Spanish conquistadores as Don Juan de Oñate. Because they are pictorial narratives, at first glance Solomon's etchings would seem to have more in common with the work of Honoré Daumier or with American Social Realism of the 1930s. But in fact, Heap of Birds and Solomon share a deep interest in the violence of colonial history and in finding an effective mode of communication, as both of them are committed to audience engagement. Third, let us remember that during the Sydney Biennale in 1988, Australian Aboriginal artists installed two hundred hollow-log bone coffins that memorialized their ancestors who were killed while defending their country during the previous two centuries of colonialism. This symbolic inversion—that is, this "un-celebration" of colonial culture—was widely conceded to be the most important work of art associated with the biennale and was subsequently collected by the National Gallery of Australia in Canberra.[23] And last, the Santa Clara Pueblo artist Nora Naranjo-Morse recently finished an inspiring environmental landscape titled *Numbe Whageh (Our Center Place)* at the Albuquerque Museum, which offers a Native response to the Cuarto Centenario observance of Don Juan de Oñate's arrival in New Mexico.[24] This list could be much longer, so suffice it to say that *Wheel* does not live in isolation but is part of an important body of international contemporary artworks that bring to light that which is all too often buried, but which is always extant in traumatic memory.

## Notes

1. See also W. Jackson Rushing III, "In Our Language: The Emergence of Edgar Heap of Birds," *Third Text* 19 (July 2005): 365–84.

2. In the late 1970s and early 1980s he made provocative, if ungainly, word/image paintings and gradually determined to separate the organic shapes (which grew into *Neuf* imagery) from the words. On artists using words since the 1980s, see Tony Godfrey, *Conceptual Art* (London: Phaidon, 1998), 343–76. See also my essay "Street Chiefs and Native Hosts: Richard Ray (Whitman) and Edgar Heap of Birds Defend the Homeland," in *Green Acres: Neo-Colonialism in the United States,* ed. Christopher Scoates (St. Louis: Washington University Gallery of Art, 1992), 31.

3. Hal Foster, ed., *The Anti-Aesthetic: Essays on Postmodern Culture* (Port Townsend, WA: Bay Press, 1983), xv.

4. See Craig Owens, "Improper Names," *Art in America,* October 1986, 129.

5. Edgar Heap of Birds, quoted in Jamake Highwater, "Heap of Birds," *Native Arts/West,* April 1981, 31. See also both his statement "Of Circularity and Linearity in the Work of Bear's Heart," and my essay "The Legacy of Ledger Book Drawings in Twentieth-Century Native American Art," in *Plains Indian Drawings 1865–1935: Pages from a Visual History,* ed. Janet Catherine Berlo (New York: Harry N. Abrams, 1996), 66 and 56–62.

6. According to Holliday T. Day, the artist "surmises that the name Many Magpies recalled the entire visual image and mood of a certain time of day when these birds gathered, rather than a limited designation of his great-great grandfather as a pile of

birds"; see "*He says, She says*" (Omaha, NE: Joslyn Art Museum, 1982), n.p.

7. Brochure for *Sharp Rocks*, a solo exhibition at Artculture Resource Center in Toronto, Ontario, 1987.

8. Edgar Heap of Birds, "Insurgent Messages for America," *Afterimage* 14 (October 1986); reprinted in *Claim Your Color*, Papo Colo et al. (New York: Exit Art, 1989), 22.

9. For Jean-Michel Basquiat and SAMO, see Richard Marshall, *Jean-Michel Basquiat* (New York: Whitney Museum of American Art, 1993), 16.

10. Edgar Heap of Birds, artist's statement in *Word/Image: The Art of Reading*, by Barrett Watten (San Francisco: New Langston Art, 1985), 14. Cf. my comments in "Street Chiefs," 31–32.

11. Joan Rothfuss, statement issued in conjunction with *Building Minnesota* (1990). Some of my comments on this installation first appeared in "Street Chiefs," 33.

12. Edgar Heap of Birds, statement for *Building Minnesota*, in *Caliban* 8 (1990): 81.

13. Heap of Birds, in *Claim Your Color*, 22.

14. Andrea Miller-Keller, "Dunging the Ground," in *Hachivi Edgar Heap of Birds: MATRIX 131*, ed. Andrea Miller-Keller (Hartford, CT: Wadsworth Atheneum Museum of Art, 1996), 4–5.

15. Artist's statement in *Hachivi Edgar Heap of Birds: MATRIX 131*, 2.

16. Ibid.

17. Ibid.

18. Ibid.

19. Heap of Birds, in *Claim Your Color*, 22.

20. Ibid.

21. Lee-Ann Martin, "Indigenous Renewal = Reclamation + Redefinition = Reality = Identity," in *16 Songs: Issues of Personal Assessment and Indigenous Renewal*, Diana R. Block and Edgar Heap of Birds (Denton, TX: University of North Texas Art Gallery, 1995), 7.

22. Edgar Heap of Birds, unpublished proposal for *Wheel* (1998), courtesy of the artist.

23. See John Mundine, "Aboriginal Art in Australia Today," *Third Text* 6 (Spring 1989): 40–42.

24. See Nora Naranjo-Morse, *Numbe Whageh (Our Center Place)*. One videocassette (10 minutes), 2005; distributed by Vtape, Toronto.

Fig. 41    *The North American Iceberg,* 1985
Carl Beam
Acrylic, photo-serigraph, and graphite
on Plexiglass, 84 × 147¼ in.
Photo © National Gallery of Canada, Ottawa

There are somewhere around two thousand art galleries and museums across Canada, everything from small-town and county museums to multimillion-dollar city, provincial, and national art galleries and museums. In the United States, the American Association of Museums estimates that there are 17,500 museums and galleries. With so many of these institutions in both countries in the hands of non-Indians, which is to say, people who often know little to nothing about Native Americans and First Nations peoples, the easy answer to the question of whether or not the segregation of Native art by ethnicity is self-imposed or superimposed would seem to be self-evident—it would be superimposed. But this is a loaded question, since what may appear self-evident historically is not necessarily the case contemporaneously. At the Denver Art Museum, for instance, where the museum prides itself on a splendid collection of Native art, the answer seems clear that any segregation by ethnicity here is obviously superimposed, that is, when looked at historically. And unless someone can prove to me that Native artists have had a fundamental part in designing the concept of this institution from the ground up, that does seem to be the case. On the other hand, you do not see Native artists or activists protesting how the DAM is exhibiting the art today. To the contrary, that fact that Native Americans are mute on this question implies a certain acceptance of the status quo—so the answer could just as well be that segregation is self-imposed, if segregation it is.

However, if you ask whether segregation is a positive or negative experience for the Native artist, I would say segregation alone does not necessarily guarantee a negative or positive response since, as you can see, the answer must always be provisional—it depends on who is doing the asking, the looking, and the critical analysis, and who is feeling accepted or isolated. Whereas a Native artist might feel a certain acceptance at being included in a mainstream art gallery such as the National Gallery of Canada as an

# Segregation of Native Art by Ethnicity
# Is It Self-imposed or Superimposed?
*by Alfred Young Man*

Fig. 42   *Observations of the Astral World,* c. 1994
Norval Morrisseau
Acrylic on canvas, 92⅞ × 202⅜ × 1½ in.
© Norval Morrisseau / Gabe Vadas, courtesy of Kinsman Robinson
Galleries, Toronto; Photo © National Gallery of Canada, Ottawa

"Artist" with a capital A, and therefore the artist sees segregation as having ended; on the other hand, the Native art historian may feel rejection, isolation, and an imposed segregation; both professions are a vital and essential part of what I call the eight components, or "hoop," of Indian fine arts: artist, historian/scholar, curator, publisher, gallery, collector, bookstore, and academic. Currently only a few Native artists have been accepted by the mainstream art establishment as Artists with a capital A; therefore, in the eyes of the gallery at least, these individual artists have won or earned the Western art establishment's stamp of approval; in other words, they have been validated by those who have the power to validate, effectively breaking the hoop of Native art.

Let me play devil's advocate for a moment: the National Gallery of Canada (NGC) in Ottawa had more than 650,000 visitors pass through its doors in 2004. How much Native art did those patrons of art see? The answer is very little, and for a couple of solid reasons. Primarily, the tiny collection of Native art at the NGC is sparsely exhibited in that old institution. Its comparatively new digs opened in 1988 (the gallery itself was established in 1880). Because the purchasing and exhibiting of Native art—or if you prefer, art done by artists of Native ancestry—is a relatively new phenomenon for the NGC, progress is slow, as it has been for most Western art galleries and institutions that deal exclusively with Euro-American artists, or artists of Western culture and worldview.

The serious business of collecting contemporary Native art by the National Gallery of Canada began around 1987 with the purchase of the late Carl Beam's *North American Iceberg* (Fig. 41), as recommended by curator Diana Nemiroff. From February 3 to April 30, 2006, a retrospective of Objiwe artist Norval Morrisseau's paintings (Fig. 42) was on view at the NGC, so the gallery has come a long way—or short way depending on how you view this argument—

since 1880, which is a space of 126 years. Historically, the NGC began as a colonialist British institution built to celebrate art created by recent British and then European immigrants to the new country called Canada. Its original policy and goal were certainly not to collect Native art per se, nor is it an avowed strategy today. To paraphrase Lynda Jessup in her essay "Hard Inclusion," art galleries that practice exclusion are simply adhering to the century-old Canadian practice of ensuring that their powerful ideological spaces are reserved for Western aesthetics or settler art.[1] Then too, as Nemiroff once said, "I'm interested in looking at the work of individuals . . . I don't particularly look at the work of a group of artists as blocks of certain types, like Native artists, or woman artists, or French Canadian artists. I don't usually use those categories."[2] In the minds of the people at the NGC, then, obviously (or perhaps not) the collecting and exhibiting of Native art as "Native art" is better left to national museums of nature and anthropology, such as the National Museum of Man, now renamed the Canadian Museum of Civilization (CMC), which is situated on the north bank of the Ottawa River in Hull, Quebec, almost directly across from the NGC. Ironically, that river is a symbolic, historical, and physical barrier to Native art ever being shown at the NGC as "Native art writ large," that is, Native art that incorporates the eight components I mentioned before (artist, historian/scholar, curator, publisher, gallery, collector, bookstore, and academic). Meanwhile at the CMC, Native art is openly exhibited as "primitive art" created by Canadian Indians, or First Nations if you prefer, never to be referred to as art writ large—a clear case of superimposed segregation that is based on a case of mistaken identity. I know that some of you may disagree with this statement, but it is grounded in the facts of Euro-Canadian and American history and anthropology.

At first, back in 1989, in its newly minted building, the NGC displayed its also newly acquired small collection of contemporary Native art in a gallery all by itself. This bold move, I unwisely and wrongly assumed, meant that Native art history too had finally arrived, was finally being taken seriously, was being acknowledged and accepted by the art establishment in Canada. It is common wisdom that the NGC first began collecting Native art around 1987 with the purchase of that work by Beam, and then that it purchased new works for the collection as time passed.[3] Anyway, some members of the Native art community voiced some rather vocal and heated complaints about the perceived "ghettoization" of their work, being exhibited in its own room, as it were, or gallery at the NGC. They alleged that the NGC was giving Native artists their own "rez." Because of that stinging criticism, the gallery determined to disperse the collection throughout the general "prison" population, as I call it. The net effect of this move was to ensure that Native artists and their history were once again emasculated, marginalized, and made invisible to all but the most astute and knowledgeable of the Native art-going public among us, who are few in number. From the perspective of the Native art historian then, this was clearly another case of superimposition, since the NGC was now not only *not* going to recognize these First Nations and Native American artists as the people they were culturally and historically, but by proxy they were doing this with the blessing of the Native artists themselves, hell-bent on obliterating the history of Native art altogether. Assimilation by any other name, in other words.

How many patrons who viewed Native art at the NGC after it was dispersed throughout the galleries even knew that they were looking at the art of a Native artist when they crossed a particular painting's path? With little information to guide them—and in keeping with NGC policy just the name of the artist, maybe the year of birth and death, the medium, size, title of the work, the year it was created, and perhaps the donor's name being displayed—

how was a viewer to know that the person who did the art was a Native person? Add to this confusing situation that, depending on the style of the artwork and medium, a viewer could now inexplicably come across the artwork of Cree artist Allen Sapp displayed alongside art by early Canadian landscape painters, or artwork by Dene artist Alex Janvier (Fig. 43) exhibited adjacent to the work of abstract expressionists with no explanation at all about the work, periods, or even eras. Identifying these Native artists as contemporaneous with styles and artists—some who lived and died before the Native artists in question were even born or working as artists—seems bizarre. There is no attempt made to associate the work, its style, its derivativeness, or provenance with the Native nation or culture the artist heralded from. The entire exercise is one of futility and seems odd given an otherwise sterling reputation and record of documenting the national and personal histories of artists of other races, nations, or types of artwork. To compare two artists in the collection, for instance, we know that Andy Warhol was Polish American and that life in the United States, in Pittsburgh specifically, deeply influenced his life as an artist. But does John Q. Public know that Lawrence Paul Yuxweluptun (Fig. 44) is Salish or how deeply his people's history influences his work? Enough has been written and published on Warhol so that the average gallery visitor can place Warhol's work in some sort of historical and cultural context, but with very little written on Yuxweluptun, or any of the other Native artists in the collection for that matter, the visitor is at pains to readily contextualize Native artists in Canadian history. In short, more work needs to be done in researching, writing, publishing, and giving gallery space over to Native art history.

Clearly, this is one instance where First Nations people should have left well enough alone and simply kept to the original idea of a homogeneous gallery, since the history

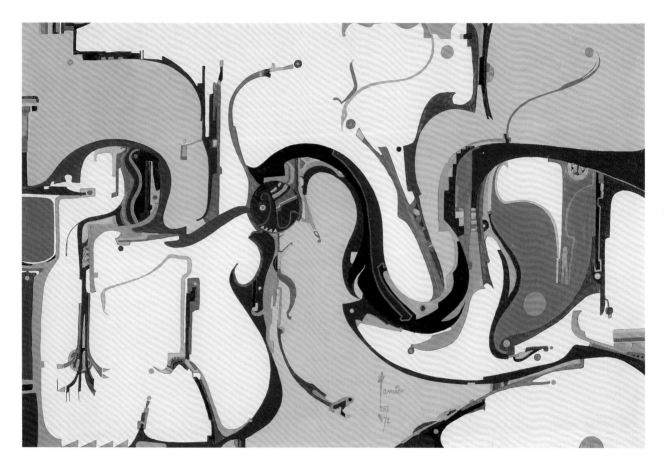

Fig. 43  *Coming of the Opposite,* 1972
Alex Janvier
Acrylic on canvas, 24⅛ × 36⅜ in.
Photo © National Gallery of Canada, Ottawa

Fig. 44    *The Universe is so Big, the White Man Keeps Me on My Reservation,* 1987
Lawrence Paul Yuxweluptun
Acrylic on canvas, 72 × 89¾ in.

would have at least had some little opportunity to flourish in that environment. And if the actions of the Native artists who protested against being given their own gallery at the NGC can now be called a self-imposed kind of segregation because they are losing their connection with Native art history (which in my view as a Native art historian is just another form of superimposed segregation), then perhaps history is worth segregating oneself for. At least Native art would gain some measure of recognition and resist assimilation into nothingness, as is now happening at the NGC. The question of whether that gallery of Native art was meant to be a permanent exhibition in homage to Native art and its history or if it was merely a temporary installation is one that I have not had the pleasure of asking Ms. Nemiroff. The answer, most likely, is the latter, which would change my argument but not by much. Unfortunately, if a Native art student or scholar wants to research Native art history, the NGC is clearly not the place to go, since its avowed policy is to collect and exhibit only art made by artists who claim no "ethnic" background, to purchase only art that has been made for art's sake, whatever that is—the *art for art's sake* slogan. Defining the word "ethnic" is also an important issue, because in my view, North American Indians are not an ethnic group in the same way that American or Canadian Irish, Scots, Italians, Russians, and so forth practice what they call their ethnicity, at least not in the typical usage of the word as conceived by the Eurocentric mind.

While the unilateral practice by Nemiroff of collecting the "individual" as artist may seem like an admirable practice to some, ultimately this attitude, when applied to Native art, is nothing more than a diplomatic way of saying that if you are an Indian who insists on working as the Native artist you are, well, you need not apply for the gig. The problem goes much deeper than that of course. What they are really saying is "no Indians or Indian art allowed,

just the artist," whatever that means. You may want to know that one definition of a diplomat that I have heard is that a diplomat can tell you to go to hell and make you like it.

## Anthropologists and Other Friends

In 1969, in the chapter "Anthropologists and Other Friends" in *Custer Died for Your Sins,* the late Standing Rock Sioux author Vine Deloria Jr. wrote, "Into each life, it is said, some rain must fall. Some people have bad horoscopes, others take tips on the stock market. McNamara created the TFX and the Edsel, Churches possess the real world. But Indians have been cursed above all other people in history. Indians have anthropologists."[4]

Anthropology has never quite recovered from that battle cry, and the resulting relationship between anthros and Indians has never quite been the same. Deloria would move on to write or edit other influential books that were in part critical of the anthropological profession, including *We Talk, You Listen: New Tribes, New Turf* (1970); *God Is Red: A Native View of Religion* (1972); *The Metaphysics of Modern Existence* (1979); *Red Earth, White Lies: Native Americans and the Myth of Scientific Fact* (1995); *Indians and Anthropologists: Vine Deloria, Jr. and the Critique of Anthropology* (1997); and *Spirit and Reason: The Vine Deloria, Jr., Reader* (1999).

In "Civilization and Isolation," an impressive paper delivered at Athabasca University's Edmonton campus in 1977—a paper that would go on to reign as the last word in Native epistemology on the question of anthropology and Western discourse in general—Deloria delivered his seminal and most critical presentation on the question of Western vs. North American Indian knowledge. *The Metaphysics of Modern Existence* would be the result of his thinking up to that time. In his lecture and later in his book, Deloria laid out the basic premises and differences between the Native and Western perspectives, ultimately labeling

Western thinking as provincial and parochial with regard to its interpretation and understanding of time and space, or better yet, its misunderstanding of Native peoples' understanding of culture, history, time, space, and reason, and moreover his analysis of the wholesale acceptance by Western thinkers of anthropological theory and concepts regarding North American Indians. The late Lakota anthropologist Bea Medicine would characterize anthropology as engaging in the study of an "ethnographic present" type of Indian, meaning that, in effect, anthropologists were studying a nonexistent personage, someone who fit their ideas of what an Indian was supposed to be. I sometimes think that there must be some kind of anthropologically defined "super Indian" out there waiting in the wings, ready to pounce on the real Native artists, academics, and scholars who are critical of that social science profession.

The relationship between anthropology and the First Nations peoples and Native Americans of Canada and the United States has been problematic for more than one hundred fifty years, to the point that reserves and reservations in both countries refuse to allow anthros onto their land to conduct their fieldwork, at least not without packing around a hard-won resolution from a band or tribal council allowing them onto the rez. Part of the problem with answering the question about the segregation of Native art can be laid squarely at the feet of anthropology. It would take more than this essay to fully analyze that uneasy relationship, so I will not go there this time around. Instead, it is important that we focus on the role that anthropology has played in the definition of Native art and how that description influences the negative practices and policies of the Canadian, American, European, and world art establishments toward Native art through time. With that condition in mind, I will further narrow my focus to the perennial question of where Native art is to be "positioned" in the white art mainstream. And because

the narrative, the discourse, still largely belongs to the Western art and scientific disciplines to do with as they please, this approach would seem to be a valid one. Anthropology has certainly played a central role in determining where Native art "belongs" in the mainstream institutions of Western civilization this past century. Ironically, the gridlock that Native art is experiencing today should not have to happen to what are arguably the most studied people on the planet, but the gridlock is there nevertheless. That, in addition to having to acknowledge that Native art is a multibillion-dollar industry, makes the question of segregation seem a complete obscenity. And then, too, trying to unravel the problem of "positioning" at this late date in history seems utterly illogical since the answer should be as self-evident as the nose on your face. I think that what we have here is simply a question of bald-faced politics running rampant over art. The art is there and always has been; the question is, how do we get that art into the gallery via the front door? How do we connect the pieces of the puzzle?

## Early Beginnings

Part of the answer to this symbiotic question extends back to the early years of the twentieth century, when European and American artists first noticed that North American Indians could create artistic, creative, inventive, beautiful, and expressive art objects for their own sake—art for art's sake. The Western idea of aesthetics did not exist in the American Indian worldview at first, although Native artists invariably arrived at the answer to how aesthetics functioned in their daily lives anyway, using means other than those commonly understood and practiced by Western academics. Obviously, North American Indians did not need Western conversation to tell them what was good in their art. They already knew what worked and what did

Fig. 45    *Head of a Sleeping Woman
(Study for Nude with Drapery),*
Paris, summer 1907
Pablo Picasso (1881–1973)
Oil on canvas, 24¼ × 18¾ in.
Estate of John Hay Whitney (278.1983); © 2007
Estate of Pablo Picasso/Artists Rights Society (ARS),
New York; Digital Image © The Museum of Modern
Art / Licensed by SCALA / Art Resource, NY

not, which made it possible for white artists like Pablo
Picasso (Fig. 45) and Marcel Duchamp to pontificate about
how these fascinating objects they called Indian art were to
be classified. What sort of thinking brought these things to
fruition? Picasso would never come to realize in its totality,
however, what sort of thinking produced American Indian
art because all he wanted to know was how the outer form
was constructed, not how its inner content was informed
by "tribal" knowledge. He is rumored to have said, "All that
I need to know about this Northwest Coast mask is right
here in the mask"—or some such thing. Of course, such
minuscule knowledge would not afford him much knowledge at all of Northwest Coast Indians. Classification in
those early years, and not how the art was made, became
the issue among anthropologists and academics, and it
still is the issue a century later. It seems to me that our task
today is to do away with those classifications entirely and
replace them with something more appropriate to who we
are today. These first white specialists were people who
were still comparatively innocent in their knowledge of
how this new idea called "modernism" would function
in society. It was not too long before that, that this new
idea called "art writ large" was invented in the mid-1800s.
The first-ever seriously written critique of something we
now call "art" is still out there somewhere. That document
should be tracked down, preserved, and put on display
in some museum somewhere, perhaps alongside the Dead
Sea Scrolls.

    Diana Nemiroff wrote in *Land, Spirit, Power: First
Nations at the National Gallery of Canada* that the issue of
positioning Native art, that is literally where to put Native
art in the gallery, has made an on-and-off-again appearance
with the national and international art institutions of
Canada and the United States since 1927, when "a growing
number of exhibitions in Europe and the United States in
the nineteen-tens and -twenties . . . sought to demonstrate

an elective affinity between the tribal and modern, in so doing accorded non-Western objects an honorary place in Western art history."[5] The question of having an "honorary" place was not settled once and for all in 1927. Much later, in October 1978, at the first-ever Canadian national gathering of First Nations artists, mainstream artists, curators, gallery directors, and other art professionals, hosted by the Ojibwe Cultural Foundation in West Bay, Ontario, participants debated the question for three days.[6] After that, with what has been deadening regularity, this issue of positioning has been examined again and again at virtually every national conference or symposium held on Native art from 1979 to 2005.

## All Those Symposia and Conferences

In 1979 the question of where to display Native art was raised at a symposium held at the Saskatchewan Indian Federated College on the University of Regina campus. In 1983 it was discussed again, at the Kitanmax School of Northwest Coast Indian Art at 'Ksan, in Hazelton, British Columbia. In 1987 it raised its homely head yet again at the Society of Canadian Artists of Native Ancestry (SCANA) symposium "Networking," at the University of Lethbridge, and after that, in 1988, it was still being discussed at length in the pages of *Muse* magazine.[7] At each and every one of these conferences, anthropology was present, if not in force, then in spirit, presiding over the discussions like ideological vultures guarding their banquet, as they have been labeled. In 1992 the issue was again discussed by Nemiroff, who was at that time assistant curator of contemporary art at the National Gallery of Canada, in the context of the *Land, Spirit, Power* exhibition, something that I find highly ironic since she refused to acknowledge that Native art even existed in all the prior conferences and symposia she attended. During 1993

the issue was again discussed at a symposium in Halifax, Nova Scotia, titled "A Gathering in Honour of Our Teachers, Elders, and Those Who Have Gone Before Us," and in that same year the issue also appeared in Scott Watson's article "Whose Nation?" in *Canadian Art* magazine, where it occupied center stage, perhaps prodded by all the symposia I have mentioned and the *Land, Spirit, Power* exhibition, pulled together to celebrate the five-hundredth anniversary of Columbus's "discovery" of the New World. What this tells us is that where there is funding to support Native art, you can be sure that Native art will be trotted out and displayed, always, however, in the role of the perpetually blushing bride—honorary superimposition, in other words. Interestingly enough, the point of view that critics or historians take on the subject pretty much depends on where they are geographically and politically located in North America. Significantly, in those years when Native art faces a funding drought, no one listens to the Native artists or critics—no one really cares. In Canada today there are mounds of government money for Native people and their art, so once again everyone is jumping on the bandwagon. In fact, we are now living through such a ridiculous period of funding that one of my Blood Indian friends has labeled this latest white invasion and fascination with acquiring money for Native projects as "Abro hunting." Some white academics are unabashedly looking for a brown Native face to insert into their proposals—paternalism and tokenism in other words—to ensure funding. These are projects that can run into the millions of dollars. Just the other day I was approached by an independent firm in Ottawa that wanted me to join them in a million-dollar proposal. All I had to do was sign on the dotted line. I said no, of course.

## Inclusion versus Exclusion

Perhaps the most definitive study ever undertaken on the question of inclusion or exclusion of Native art was Robert Houle and Carol Podedworny's *Mandate Study 1990–93,* in which they sent out questionnaires and noted demographics, all with an eye to getting the proverbial anthropological dog off the leg of the Indian artist.[8] More than six years later the issue was again the main topic of discussion at a Queen's University symposium titled "A Working Discussion on Aboriginal Representation in the Art Gallery." That meeting was held at two different locations on two different dates, in Toronto at the Art Gallery of Ontario and in Vancouver, British Columbia, at the Vancouver Art Gallery, March 4–5 and 24–25, 1999, respectively. Lynda Jessup and Shannon Bagg published *On Aboriginal Representation in the Gallery* as a result. The primary issue on the table at that symposium was the "soft versus hard inclusion" debate—as if there could be a difference. Like racism, exclusion, whether soft or hard, is still exclusion. At the University of Lethbridge, on December 2, 2005, the issue of segregation was again discussed at a symposium called "First Nations Symposium: Emerging Discourses," but all the attendees were First Nations curators. At each and every one of these symposia and conferences, going back to 1978, the idea that there might be such a thing as a Native art history was never acknowledged or discussed. I have no doubt that the problem at hand has been discussed and written about in many more times and places than what I have listed here, because it is a problem that seems to have a permanent loyal following, not only in the art community but in anthropology as well.

I think it is clear by now that this issue of segregation was first contemplated more than eight decades ago, which if you think about it, is really a lifetime of thinking and talking about Native art but a failure to consider the other components of art writ large. We would seem to require the other components of the Native art circle to come into play to complete the concept, or idea. Under the current circumstances, Native artists appear to be great innovators but never quite live up to the role or task of becoming an artist with a capital A. Native artists have only recently found themselves to be front and center in the Venice Biennale, and we still have yet to see the fruits of those appearances permanently installed at the Tate Modern in London or the Museum of Modern Art in New York City as Native art, or on permanent exhibition in any of a score of world-class art galleries and museums. Hell, we have yet to see the first published Native art book researched and written by a Native scholar from the Native perspective, so we have a long way to go.

## Reductionism

The question of reductionism is certainly in evidence at the University of Lethbridge's "Art Now" speakers' series, where artists from throughout Canada's mainstream are routinely invited to speak as visiting artists—and this includes some Native artists as well—and who are then given the keys to the city, so to speak. Not surprisingly, it seems that we are all being socially and psychologically deprived, moving backward through time to the conservative 1950s, when Native people were being relocated off the rez in the United States and told that it was okay to move into vocations such as auto mechanic, janitor, beautician, electrician, chef, plumber, laborer, or foreman, but "don't tell anyone that you're an Indian!" Similarly, the Canadian art establishment has long recited the mantra of art for art's sake, insisting that art for art's sake is the important thing, not national or "tribal"—for lack of a better word—identity, at least insofar as Native artists are concerned. In the process, Native art history is—to say it

Fig. 46    *Killer Whale,* 2000
Robert Davidson
Acrylic on canvas, 30 × 40 in.

one more time—blatantly ignored, and in so doing, Native peoples are subtly being told that their history is not important. Similarly, anthropology has a history of flatly refusing to recognize those obviously original, contemporary Native artists who are tangential to the "traditional" art that anthros have collected within their institutions, because contemporary Native art does not fit squarely into some anthropologically prescribed theory or formula. It is perhaps a little bit easier for anthropology to make the necessary connections between the traditional formline art of the early twentieth-century Haida carvers with the contemporary art created by Haida artist Robert Davidson (Fig. 46) than it is for them to make the required correlation between the traditional art of the early twentieth-century Woodland Indians with art being made today by

Chippewa artist James Havard (Fig. 47) or Oji-Cree performance artist Rebecca Belmore (Fig. 48). The dichotomy between the latter is just too great an issue for anthros to get the public and themselves to negotiate, and this is where the Native art historian plays that important role of being the connector between the two, for it is in the history that we are able to make the necessary link. Cultural content, anthropology's forte you might say, contains too many roadblocks to expect that discipline to overcome the issue of positioning all by itself. The art and anthropological establishments make no mention of the fact that while white artists get to keep their national, ethnic, and cultural identities and pride, they expect that Native artists must shed theirs, to either conform or disappear, a clear case of superimposition of ideology over history and using ethnicity to segregate once again. This is an unhealthy position for any artist to be in, Native or not. It is assimilation no matter what you call it. There seems to be a limited capacity for the status quo to digest such basic truths.

Fig. 47    *Portrait,* 2006
James Havard
Oil and wax on board,
26¼ × 20¾ in.

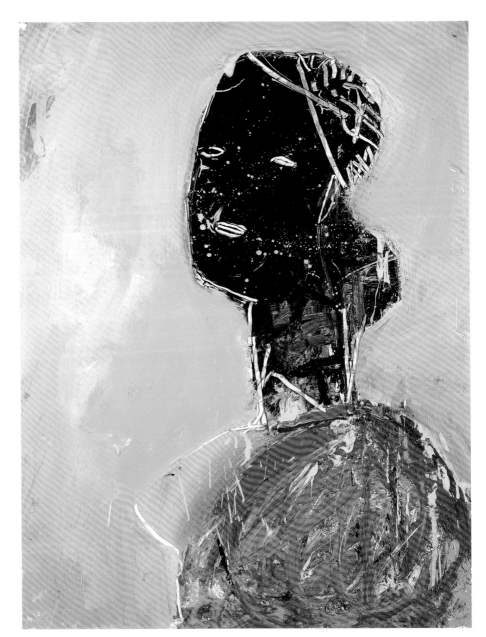

Fig. 48    *Ayum-ee Aawach Oomama-mowan:*
           *Speaking to Their Mother,* 1991
           Rebecca Belmore
           Mixed media installation, performance

## Assimilation and Appropriation

Anne Newlands's glossy coffee-table book titled *Canadian Art: From Its Beginnings to 2000* does a wonderful job of appropriating Native artists into the Canadian art historical mainstream, in hopes that perhaps by directly assimilating Native artists into the larger national consciousness, the more complex and difficult question of positioning will somehow be forever answered—"so let us just get on with making real art and stop this political nonsense!" Admittedly, it is completely legitimate for Native artists to complain about having to identify themselves and their art as belonging to the First Nations or Native art classification—this does carry with it some very heavy and unwanted political and cultural baggage, as I have been saying for most of this essay, but then, that is one of the issues that makes Native art "Native art." Obviously, being labeled an "ethnic" artist by the art establishment is beneath the dignity of what real, sincere art writ large is supposed to be all about. As if to underscore this point, a symposium sponsored by Queen's University raised the following issue regarding strategies for assimilating Native art and artists into the mainstream art galleries and getting out of the anthropological quagmire:

> At present, Aboriginal historical cultures are represented almost exclusively in Euro-Canadian painting, sculpture, and graphics in the Canadian historical wing of the Art Gallery of Ontario and the Canadian installations at the Vancouver Art Gallery. One strategy for effecting change and for securing Aboriginal cultures a presence at the AGO is the introduction of early Woodlands material in exhibition spaces of Euro-Canadian art of the same period and region, including early work produced for the Euro-Canadian market. Historical examples of basketry and weaving from among Pacific Coast

Aboriginal peoples, similarly, might find a place in the Vancouver Art Gallery in the same way contemporary pieces by Rena Point Bolton and Isabel Rorick appeared in the VAG's 1996 show, *Topographies: Aspects of Recent B.C. Art*. Among the many challenges posed by this idea is the introduction of what have been called tourist art and craft traditions into the gallery setting.[9]

The point here about strategies of assimilation is a complex one indeed, but my argument has always been that the supposed difficulties of incorporating Native fine art into the national scene at a high standard are largely illusory since all art, on a planetary scale anyway, can be qualified to some degree as ethnic art or as being something less than truly universal anyway. With Native art of a sufficiently high standard, the problem is even more of an illusion. Picasso, after all, is of the old modernist convention of painting *and* he is a Spanish artist, yet no one is getting their shorts tied in a knot arguing over whether or not his ethnic or national identity should be abolished or questioned. How ethnic and non-universal is that? What about Andy Warhol? He was a Polish American artist. Even the Canadian Group of Seven are not taken seriously by the Museum of Modern Art in New York City as completely universal in their outlook, since they are doing something called "Canadian" art. The issue has always been a purely political one. In their textbooks, Western art historians in the United States have completely ignored the fact that there is something called a Canadian art history, so Canadians have something in common with ignored Native artists. One has to specifically study Canadian art history before one even learns that the Group of Seven painters existed (one might say they are the most Canadian of all Canadian artists). The 1969 edition of the *McGraw-Hill Dictionary of Art* makes no mention at all of the Group of Seven, although the list of Western art and artists is extensive, listing everything from the paintings on the walls of the caves of Lascaux to the frescoes of Hellenic Greece to the Renaissance to pop art to minimalism, in five big volumes, and those books are on the shelves forever.[10] Unless art history has made a fundamental turnabout in the past three decades and has been completely rewritten, how can we say that there is such a thing as a "universal" art in Canada? Obviously, if there was such a thing then why would postmodernism—which is anything but universal—need to be invented? This is a purely political question.

When I was a student at the Slade School of Fine Art, University College, London, from 1968 to 1972, we were forbidden to study paintings and sculptures created by communist Russian, Chinese, or Vietnamese artists. No gallery or museum in England would dare to show such work. The line was that communists were unable to do art writ large, that their work was highly political and therefore it was to be taken as sheer propaganda. Today, at the Tate Modern in London, a visitor can go into the galleries and appreciate all kinds of Russian and Chinese communist "political" art (Fig. 49), displayed as art writ large. So what happened there?

William E. Taylor naively wrote over a quarter century ago, in his foreword to *"Bo'jou, Neejee!"*:

> Canada was offered a hard, clear lesson in the costs of cultural colonialism and ethnocentrism in the nineteenth century. Yet, to this day, it seems not to have been well learned. Still struggling with the ghost of our colonial past, confusing chauvinism with nationalism while aspiring to an international image, we often underrate our richness, variety and achievements. If Canadians are characteristically critical of their own performance, let it be

Fig. 49    *Red Moscow Heart of World Revolution,* 1921
Vkhutemas (Higher State Artistic and Technical Workshops)
Ink on paper, 29⅛ × 19¾ in.

remembered that an increasing number seek to achieve a better balance.[11]

The struggle to achieve better recognition of Canada's cultural richness and diversity still continues today, if with some degree of nervousness and lack of integrity, but not by nearly enough.

## A Great Change of Consciousness Is Needed

So what, if anything, does all this confusion actually signify today anyway? This is a continuing political and historical conflict, and we have to wonder if Canada will ever be able to get it right, to be able to grasp the rich diversity, history, and variety of First Nations Native art and artists and articulate what this diversity has actually given to modernism and continues to give to postmodernism. New ways of exploring aesthetics, freedom of expression, design, shape and form, art theory and philosophy, psychology and ecology, performance art and the dramatic arts, are but a few elements in this vast paradigm called Native art, and the subject matter of that art is and will be called anthropology, is called contemporary art, is postmodernism—and all that is also forward-looking. When is the larger Western art world ever going to acknowledge this fact as it is intended, without all that meddlesome interpretation? Probably it never will, but then again, merely leaving the problem to be solved by hypothesis-spinning anthropologists in the Canadian Museum of Civilization or to superior-cogitating, Native-art-appropriating white curators to codify is probably not the answer either, if we have learned anything at all from our long history. My personal feeling is that it will take a great change of consciousness before this question of Native art writ large is going to be able to make that fundamental metamorphosis from one paradigm to another,

whatever that paradigm currently is. I do not believe, at the present time, that the Canadian, American, and European art worlds are capable of making such an all-encompassing shift on their own, at least not without the wisdom and guidance of Native artists and academics. Will Native art writ large ever be seen at the Tate Modern in London or the Museum of Modern Art in New York City?

The great amount of energy that Native artists have spent and continue to spend on solving the riddle of Native art writ large will not diminish soon. Certainly, for a people who have spent so much time and energy creating vast and ancient civilizations in the Western hemisphere for so many millennia, such a question is not an insoluble one and given their longevity in this world, it is clear that Native peoples have an endless slate of time with which to educate the postmodern world and the worlds thereafter. A fundamental paradigm shift of what Native art writ large is, or what it may yet become, may indeed be on its way (as Nemiroff suggested was supposed to have happened in 1992); however, with 20/20 hindsight I think it may not happen in my lifetime or yours, but it will surely come, for there is nowhere else to turn. With the great changes we are seeing in the fusion of Native art, dance, theater, music, performance art, drama, poetry, and literature with that of Western culture's contemporary art, rock and classical music, cinema, and so forth, the change is bound to happen, for it is happening all around us as we speak. Rock stars who were once fearful to admit to their First Nations and Native American identities are now coming out of the closet. Musicians like Rita Coolidge, the late Johnny Cash, and Robbie Robertson have admitted fraternity in the society of these so-called primitive peoples. How would it affect Native art history if Robert Rauschenberg finally admits to his rumored Cherokee roots? The Group of Seven had one of their number admit to being a Métis. People such as these can safely be labeled "closet Indians" for all intents and purposes, but their addition to the world of Native art and cultural history is most welcome. All that we need agree to do is find a way to suitably categorize Native art by historical title, as was accomplished with naming the Canadian Indian Fine Art Movement in the 1990s. We need a universal agreement that there is such a thing as Native art history and a better way to classify the contemporary versus the traditional, perhaps to do away with the term *traditional* altogether, for by one account we are the traditional. Who knows, the required terminology may yet be coined at some future conference, in some academic forum or perhaps even in some bar, where these matters are hotly debated among Native artists, poets, writers, entertainers, and the philosophers of the world. All we need do is get the ball rolling with a catchy name, title, phrase, or buzzword, and the rest will take care of itself. I mean, whoever heard of postmodernism before the 1970s? Whoever heard of "the gaze" before the 1960s? What about soft versus hard inclusion?

### Native Art as Art Writ Large

The idea of art writ large, then, in the Western sense, is an idea that can be argued to good effect by anybody in any culture who feels that they can make a strong enough case for any sort of unique political, historical, patriotic, cultural, scientific, or even religious circumstances that may have given birth to a particular art form or movement; in other words, to make what might be perceived as a valid argument for art writ large in those cases. All that a Western art critic or historian needs is a bit of common sense and a place to stand, and—theoretically anyway—he or she could move the world. In the case of the art theory shifts of indigenous peoples, I find it useful to assert oneself primarily from the spatially and temporally different Native perspective, for that is where the basic intellectual and philosophical consciousness and content resides by which

any cutting-edge art criticism or history of Native art can be made. Furthermore, when a Native critic or historian is arguing purposefully for the paradigm "Native art," the narrative used to normally assert the supremacy of art writ large from a Western perspective does not automatically disappear and become inoperative simply because the conversation has shifted to that experience which is deemed indigenous in scope and origin. Such a pessimistic attitude, although widely held, is simplistic and unrealistic to the extreme. The theory of art writ large truly is a curious phenomenon because it is a universal question; therefore it must be of a polemical nature and manifest from any perspective . . . it cannot be construed to serve just the narrow intents and confines of an otherwise dilettantish Western art world, or rather when it does, it does so unwillingly.

### The Problem of Victorian Taxonomy and the Beginnings of Modernism via Anthropology

The segregation issue is all bound up with the historical classification of Native people in those public anthropological and art institutions that depend on a Victorian classification system for their very survival. Take away the current classification of Canadian Indian art from the Canadian Museum of Civilization and what have you got left? The museum would die, virtually overnight. If this question of inclusion versus exclusion had been asked of any other art movement in Canada, I dare say a solution would have been found by now. This obfuscation has such an enduring quality about it that it has now become a permanent ingredient in the collective unconscious of all those who discuss Native art on a regular basis: institutional racism by any other name. Deloria had great fears that the parochial nature of Western scientific thought would become a permanent feature in the way Native people view time and space, and he sought to make sure that such would not be the case. I believe that in Western art, it already has become the case. And if that is indeed true then how will there ever be a lasting conclusion to this enigmatic problem? As you can see, the question has been bandied about and otherwise reviewed, revised, analyzed, scrutinized, criticized, judged, and evaluated by nearly everyone from museum directors and curators to artists, anthropologists, ethnographers, critics, academics, scholars, students, politicians, and even the man on the street, taking up billions of tons of paper and billions more gigabytes per decade than any environmental impact statement ever could. Lately, the issue seems to have become political fodder for those philistines in academia who are resisting altogether the idea of Native art writ large acquiring a history for itself, those who would rather that the issue simply go away. Like it or not, Western academics perceive segregation to be an irresolvable political question because they know so little about Native art. Typically, what you do not understand you tend to ignore, so they are doing their best to ignore it, that is until someone comes along and pointedly prods them into looking for answers and ways to give a studied, realistic answer, and then the hand-wringing begins in earnest all over again. The current popular trend is to simply appropriate Native artists into the postmodern mainstream, shorn of any association at all with First Nations or Native American history, cultural roots, personal integrity, and intellectual content—assimilated into some great mysterious melting pot of Canadian identity, irrespective of how multicultural or pluralistic Canada claims to be. I suppose that anthropology could still serve as Native art's self-appointed savior, but on the other hand, such dubious heroism could inherently promote the suppression and repression of Native art for yet another hundred years. We have been down that road before.

In order to come to a more comprehensive understanding of where Native art is going today, or should be going, it is necessary to know and understand where we came from. Therefore, a general but succinct slice of Western art history is in order here. Modernism, and later its offspring postmodernism, owes much of its consciousness of itself— if not its complete raison d'être—to anthropology. Now, as outlandish a statement as this may at first seem, this is an undeniable fact, verifiable by historical precedent. Few academics and laymen seem to understand this basic principle of art writ large, and fewer artists and even curators are taught this history in art schools. And even if this truth is somehow seen as self-evident and understood by those few who do care enough to investigate its authenticity, it is still unlikely that they can actually wrap their minds around what this fact ultimately means in its greater implications for contemporary Native art history and theory.

Without going into a long, drawn-out treatise of where and when museums first began in North America or how anthropology gave the art world the model for its art classification system . . . briefly: in the age of Queen Victoria (the era that gave rise to ethnography and modern art) anthropologist Otis T. Mason postulated in 1894 that there were six major classes of human arts and industries: exploitation, cultivation, manufacture, transportation, commerce, and enjoyment.[12] By classifying and aligning the tools (manufacture) made by humans beginning with Stone Age tools on through the Copper, Bronze, Iron, and finally Atomic Ages, Mason deemed it possible to ascertain the "cultural status" of each race of man and to infer from this what each culture gave to the present in the way of knowledge and technology. Since the tools excavated from pre-Columbian Indian burial mounds, caves, graves, and other archaeological sites were primarily stone implements, this methodology commonly put Indian cultures at a disadvantage, landing them squarely in some distant Stone Age.

Some educators today still use a "cultural status" device to classify ethnographic theory and data as fact.[13]

Naturally, in Victorian times, the newly coined expression and paradigm, the "art of Western man," needed some sort of explanation by which to move itself forward, and the newly born discipline of anthropology just happened to provide the required epistemology by which to provide that definition, to say nothing of the fact that—as North American Indian history tells us—it was an absolutely politically expedient move. Thus, all arts and crafts created and produced by humans since humankind's earliest ancestors and all societies established by humankind since the dawn of time were classified according to Darwin's—some say Alfred Wallace's—theory of evolution, and accounted for on a scale moving from a lower plane of biological, cultural, social, intellectual, scientific, and genetic development to a supposedly higher plane, which is the theory of cultural evolution. Western civilization, that is, what was modern in the nineteenth century, represented to the people of that time the pinnacle of human achievement, whereas the classical aesthetics of the Renaissance and the Victorian age were considered to be the source of man's greatest art.[14] Perhaps retired Rutgers University anthropology professor William K. Powers summarizes the paradoxical nature of this archaic perspective best, regarding Western civilization's affectation for classifying plant and animal kingdoms according to their differences along an evolutionary time line—in human societies, hierarchically classifying the differences between arts and crafts—out of which art and anthropology originated as disciplines in their own right, effectively inventing a new paradigm for classifying the primitive versus civilized:

> Why did we develop a society that insists on arguing over the differences, since the definitions of each must always be provisional or operational? . . . It is

quite clear that the way we traditionally classify art is simply an extension of the way we classify people, and the whole scheme smacks of the classificatory system made famous by numerous social theorists living in the mid-nineteenth century. Sir Edward B. Tylor of England and Lewis Henry Morgan reflected current Victorian perceptions in seeing all of humankind as culturally evolving through three stages of development, namely savagery, a period characterized by hunting and gathering; barbarism, a period characterized by the development of agriculture and ceramic industries; and finally civilization, whose hallmark was the invention of writing. Thus we have a popular view of primitive art, folk art, and Art writ large as, in effect, structural analogs of savagery, barbarism, and civilization . . . These ideas are still very much alive among laymen, although anthropologists rejected these theories long ago.[15]

Powers goes on to write:

> It is unlikely that a new classification system, one that does not distinguish between Art writ large, and arts written with a small "a" and pluralized, will come into effect in a very short time, because we are all fortunately or unfortunately products of our own cultures and the values associated with them.[16]

So successful has this classification system been that computer word processors that utilize a thesaurus such as that used by Corel WordPerfect software give the following words as synonyms for "Native": primitive, savage, and inbred. For the word "primitive" one may find such synonyms as ancient, prehistoric, primal, aboriginal, Native, primeval, uncivilized, crude, uncultivated, unsophisticated, austere, barbarian, savage, Neanderthal, and antediluvian, among others. The Mac Word thesaurus is equally as

Fig. 50
National Gallery of Canada

refined but with an added twist, additionally listing wild, simple, rude, ignorant, idolater, coarse, barbaric, barbarous, backward, pagan, and heathen. Well, that is quite a legacy from old Victorian science, gratis anthropological theory. Regrettably, it is not only the Western world that has come to see Native people as subhuman. Through an accident of computer software, the entire planet seems to have gained the capacity to misunderstand who First Nations and Native American people are today and what we are all about. If ever there was an opportune time to change this inauspicious paradigm in the Western world for all time, it was there, in that program's thesaurus.

The National Gallery of Canada and the Canadian Museum of Civilization inherently symbolize this schism, this dichotomy between the primitive and the civilized. Certainly both institutions have long operated under such archaic assumptions in their art and ethnographic collection policies—probably from the day they opened their doors to the public. This may seem like an obvious over-generalization, but I think it may be said that the Canadian art, cultural, and scientific establishment, as a whole, has

not only openly practiced such parochial, provincial, historical, and political attitudes forever, but it continues to actively pursue and promote such choices today, thereby engendering that lasting chauvinistic character found in Canadian society as expressed by Taylor in the quote above.

## The Need for a New Native Art Classification at the National Gallery of Canada and Elsewhere

To listen to Native artists address the issue of the kind of "space" their artwork occupies at the National Gallery of Canada (Fig. 50), which is to say the way their statements are visualized by the curators as being associated with, or as coexisting with, those statements made by the more socially and politically acceptable mainstream Canadian artists, is to come to an understanding about how the complex inner workings of the Canadian art establishment function. However, traditional and contemporary Aboriginal artists do not speak with one voice on this matter either. Certainly, if we identify Inuit art as not being part of the Canadian Indian Fine Art Movement (for they do not perceive of themselves as Indians), then this division becomes even more apparent. Once I had an intense and lively conversation with Salish artist Lawrence Paul Yuxweluptun of

Fig. 51    *Rebirth of a Culture,* 1979
Daphne Odjig (b. 1919)
Acrylic on canvas, 49 × 61¼ in.
McMichael Canadian Art Collection,
donated by James Hubbard and Dennis Jones
in honour of Estella and Stuart Wright, 1991.14

Vancouver regarding how he felt about his work being hung in the National Gallery of Canada in a room with other Native artists. Not surprisingly, his response was brief and to the point. He said that the National Gallery had put him on yet another Indian reserve. He said that if he could have his way, he would rather that his work be displayed in a room with that of other Canadian artists and not in what he perceived as a segregated affair with other artists who were First Nations. I took this statement to mean that he felt that he, and they, were once again being ghettoized or marginalized by the National Gallery. With the way Native art is being categorized today, this is no doubt true.

I thoroughly sympathize with Yuxweluptun's sentiments (and I am positive that other Native artists and critics can certainly identify with his feelings as well). It is crucial to recognize first and foremost that the National Gallery is a national institution of record for everyone in Canada, not just for art produced by white Canadian artists and their history, and it should also be an honest accounting of all indigenous art, art history, and theory, and all that implies. In other words, the politically and historically autonomous Native artist and Native art historian, critic, scholar, and academic need to be publicly acknowledged and respected by that institution and not given only one room with a handful of Native artworks on display. In a country so rich and diverse in human and natural resources, surely an entire wing dedicated to the study and display of Native art and art history, critical and scholarly writings of and about the indigenous peoples of Canada, and even of North America, is possible. It goes without saying that Native peoples have an art history that spans tens of thousands of years on this continent, and Canadian nationalism should run parallel with this truth. The benefits of such an arrangement historically, culturally, politically, economically, and critically could be enormous. Any Native person, artist, art historian, critic, or

your average layperson should be able to walk up to the information desk of the National Gallery of Canada and ask for directions to the National Collection of Canadian Indian Art (or some such similar title) and be able to have easy access to a wide variety of styles, cultures, histories, mythologies, and theories as reflected in that art. The bookstore of the National Gallery should be stocking its shelves with books written by Native and non-Native academics, critics, and scholars on Native art and theory. The patron should be able to find postcards, internet links, and historical essays written on Canadian Indian art and on individual contemporary Native artists. As a Native art academic, without too much of a problem, I should be able to apply to and receive funding from Canada Council for the Arts and scores of other private, provincial, and federal granting agencies to curate exhibitions or write essays and books on Native artists who have long since passed on. This is not always possible under current national and provincial art-collecting policies. Although there are plans under way to have retrospectives in the next few years of work by Daphne Odjig (Odawa) (Fig. 51) and Alex Janvier (Dene), and a retrospective of work by Norval Morrisseau (Ojibwe) took place in 2006, there are no plans beyond these exhibitions that I know of. In addition, the NGC hired, a few years ago, a Native curator of Native art in a junior position. That position should have been a senior-level appointment.

In order to get the sort of funding I have mentioned from Canada Council, the Social Sciences and Humanities Research Council (SSHRC), or other federal granting agencies, one must be an anthropologist and then must write an essay or book based on the scientific theory that defines your subject matter rather than on how the art defines society or the land. Not surprisingly, you wind up serving the needs and ends of the status quo in a place like the Canadian Museum of Civilization. There is no good reason why retrospectives on Native artists should not be funded and held at the National Gallery on a regular basis, or why retrospectives should not be undertaken with some of Native art's most noteworthy artists while they are still alive. I should be able to do research and introduce new Native art movements and theory to the Canadian public in the National Gallery when such an idea reaches critical mass. Currently there is no such mechanism in place that will allow or lead a Native art curator or historian to do that sort of thing, except in very special circumstances such as *Land, Spirit, Power,* and it took five hundred years for that to happen. I think that this predicament shows an essential lack of imagination and political will on the part of the art and cultural establishments in Canada, that they would allow such an ambiguous situation to continue for so long. No doubt the same situation exists in the United States. How can Native artists be accused of self-imposing ethnic segregation on themselves when we have no way of reaching the pinnacle yet?

### Empowerment—All Those Museums and Galleries and Still No Place to Put Native Art?

In 1992 it was estimated that out of the two thousand museums and art galleries in Canada, there were approximately one hundred that were government-based or nationally and provincially run affairs. The remainder of the two thousand were museums of various kinds, everything from a handful of internationally known museums to large community-based museums to locally run museums and one-room displays.[17] It is safe to assume that ninety-nine percent of these sites do not address the idea of Native art writ large at all, and those that do are most likely finding the going difficult because there is no national leadership in this area. It only makes sense that the Canadian Museums

Association (CMA), the Canadian Art Museum Directors' Organization (CAMDO), Canada Council for the Arts, and the National Gallery of Canada should take a leadership role and enact collections policies and strategies that begin to seriously address this unchanging problem, and that they begin collecting art that is Native in origin for historical, cultural, political, critical, and contemporaneous reasons and make it a part of the national patrimony. This would serve two great purposes on the national and international political stages, which would bode well not only for the local community but for the country as a whole, to say nothing of the international implications. First, such a basic change in the national consciousness of a public art-collection policy would immediately place Native art, artists, curators, and art historians on an equal footing with other Canadian art professionals. Tokenism would come to an end. Native art professionals would be accepted as the Native community members they are and not as some kind of anthropologically defined, curiosity-based creature, doomed to be studied and interpreted into exclusion forever, or conversely, as some kind of Western art hybrid. Neither description is an accurate characterization of who Native art professionals are today. Native art practitioners would be seen to have viable and legitimate cultures, histories, philosophies, and a spiritual way of life that is important to the Canadian nation and world stage. In other words, they would be seen and presented as an autonomous universe in their own right, as should happen in any pluralistic, civilized society. In the end, the entire Canadian and international mosaic would benefit and be greatly strengthened. Second, achieving this goal would all but finish off the pointless idea that Native people cannot do art, have never created art, and so are forever to be consigned to the shadowy galleries of anthropology and natural history, which, while it may be good for science and bird-watchers, is not necessarily a good thing for Canada's Native people or for Canada or the world. We could then come to realize that it isn't enough to have anthropologists proclaim that their discipline had long ago rejected as nonsense those obsolete theories that were based on a dichotomous relationship between the primitive and the civilized. A corresponding movement away from, and rejection of, that old Victorian paradigm of the primitive and the civilized would need to take place in the art establishment, too, and that would require a new way of thinking and comprehending and writing about art as a whole. By empowering First Nations and Native American artists, writers, curators, art historians, and academics, that is, Native art writ large, one also empowers the people and ultimately the state. The everlasting consequences of such a move would be felt nationally and internationally and could positively influence everything in Canada and the United States from Native law to land claims to Native self-government to education to individual self-perception and motivation. It could change the state. As history reminds us, how can any so-called civilized society presume to be speaking in good faith with or about those societies that it has institutionally categorized and internalized for so long as savage and primitive—as living in a scientific, religious, historic, and political backwater—through the racist caricature, analysis, and interpretation of their philosophies, lifestyles, culture, and objects of art. In the end, superimposition itself must come to an end.

## Notes

1. Lynda Jessup, "Hard Inclusion," in *On Aboriginal Representation in the Gallery,* ed. Lynda Jessup and Shannon Bagg (Hull, Quebec: Canadian Museum of Civilization, 2002), xvi.

2. Alfred Young Man, *Networking: Proceedings from National Native Indian Artists Symposium IV* (Lethbridge, Alberta: privately published by Alfred Young Man, University of Lethbridge, 1988), 25.

3. I recently learned from Barry Ace, formerly of the Indian Art Centre (which is located in the Department of Indian Affairs and Northern Development bureaucratic headquarters in Hull) that even before Beam, the NGC had some Native art in its permanent collection that very few people knew anything about, and which work still remains a mystery.

4. Vine Deloria Jr., *Custer Died for Your Sins: An Indian Manifesto* (New York: Avon Books, 1969), 83.

5. Diana Nemiroff, Robert Houle, and Charlotte Townsend-Gault, *Land, Spirit, Power: First Nations at the National Gallery of Canada* (Ottawa: National Gallery of Canada, 1992), 20–21.

6. David General, "Indian Artists or Artists Who Are Indian?" *Native Perspective Magazine* (National Association of Friendship Centres, Ottawa) 3, no. 2 (1978): 32.

7. Robert Houle, "The Struggle against Cultural Apartheid," *Muse* (Canadian Museums Association, Ottawa), fall 1988.

8. Robert Houle and Carol Podedworny, *Mandate Study 1990–93: An Investigation of Issues Surrounding the Exhibition, Collection and Interpretation of Contemporary Art by First Nations Artists* (Thunder Bay, Canada: Thunder Bay Art Gallery, 1994).

9. Jessup and Bagg, *On Aboriginal Representation in the Gallery,* xiii.

10. Bernard S. Myers, ed., *McGraw-Hill Dictionary of Art* (New York: McGraw-Hill, 1969).

11. William E. Taylor, foreword to *"Bo'jou, Neejee!": Profiles of Canadian Indian Art* by Ted Brasser (Ottawa: National Museum of Man, 1976), 7.

12. Joan Lester, "The American Indian: A Museum's Eye View." *The Indian Historian* (Indian Historian Press, San Francisco) 5, no. 2 (1972): 3.

13. Alfred Young Man, "The Socialization and Art Politics of Native Art," Ph.D. diss., Rutgers University. UMI Dissertation Services, Ann Arbor, MI, 1997, 90.

14. Taylor, foreword to *"Bo'jou, Neejee!,"* 7.

15. William K. Powers, "Sacred Art and the Culturation of Nature," in *Beyond the Vision: Essays on American Indian Culture* (Norman, OK: University of Oklahoma Press, 1987), 77–79.

16. Ibid., 93.

17. J. Lynne Teather, "Museum-Making in Canada (to 1972)," *Muse* (Canadian Museums Association, Ottawa), summer/fall 1992, 22.

## CHAPTER 4

Do images matter? Specifically, are troublesome images, inaccurate and demeaning of racial and ethnic groups, harmless? Could all those bare-breasted warriors on horse-back and Indian princesses on cubes of margarine really have substantial material consequences? With the advent of new and more affordable technologies such as digital cameras that can instantly capture and reproduce images across the web, the proliferation of cable networks, and the absolute fluidity with which consumers recognize visual prompts (logos, brands, icons, mascots, celebrity faces), it would seem that the ability to read these conventional representations might advance beyond a literal sign-signifier level. With more images to process daily, has the American public achieved a more sophisticated level of visual literacy? Or do these signifiers continue to reproduce and reify the old one-dimensional standards of squaw and buck? What do Native people make of false representations in popular culture, and how does this impact the contemporary Native American art world?

The debates surrounding Native American representations reflect vastly different perspectives. Drawing from my research and interviews with Native artists over the past twenty years, I have identified two primary ways to think about stereotypical images—mentalist and realist. The mentalist approach dismisses stereotypes as harmless play or as inert advertisements for consumer goods, sports teams, or entertainment. Realists argue that images have consequences—bias in sports imagery, children's literature, or clothing advertisements results in psychological damage or even physical violence.

This essay is an attempt to define a critical indigenous arts theory by exposing how these divergent attitudes inform the ways we understand popular culture. My work utilizes news articles, film, photography, the internet, fine arts, academic scholarship, and, importantly, the voices of those who produce Native American imagery. I have

# A Realist View of Image Politics
## Reclamation of the "Every Indian"
### by Nancy Marie Mithlo

*After the White Man Came,* 2001
Marcus Amerman, Gwendolen Cates
Photograph, 15 × 11 in.

Fig. 52    *Land O Bucks, Land O Fakes, Land O Lakes,* 2006
David Bradley
Acrylic on paper over wood, 24 × 42 × 24 in.

chosen to focus on the perspectives and life experiences of Native women working in the arts because I find their opinions to be especially valuable in understanding communal values. A multigenerational quality of concern characterizes their viewpoints on the arts, rather than a short-term concern with economic returns only. The reader will find that I favor realist interpretations of stereotypes, advocate for collective rights, and accept the employment of stereotypes as productive tools of communication. This acceptance of the utility of false images places me in the category of a "soft" realist, for while I am troubled by stereotypes, I do not advocate total eradication of demeaning icons because of their utility and use by Indians and non-Indians as a means of conveying cultural information across divides of race and class.

Should we be concerned by the "Land O'Lakes" Indian maiden (Fig. 52) adorning our butter? Mentalists contend that there are more important things to spend capital (emotional, physical, political) on than addressing image politics. In this frame of reference, all visual references are purely cognitive and therefore ultimately inconsequential.[1] The real things that matter are economic development, political standing, and access to health care and housing. A 2006 guest columnist writing in *Indian Country Today* under the title "Free Speech: Another Side of the 'Redskin' Debate," put it this way: "I challenge all of us to put the same amount of energy (time and emotion), resources (money for lawsuits, etc.) and effort (drumming up support and blasting those not in agreement) to finding new and innovative solutions to the real reservation issues of drugs, gangs, unemployment, alcoholism, suicides, etc."[2]

A realist might counter that sexualized images of Native women do contribute to the general idea of Native women as objects—willing, available, and consumable. One needs only to look at online Halloween boutiques to see how powerfully this image gets translated into the play-acting that the American public so enjoys (the "Tribal Tease" outfit is especially telling). A quick internet search reveals that while all women might be said to be coerced into sexualized fictional roles for Halloween, Native American women in particular are singled out by ethnicity or race more often for this special appropriation. Realists can cite related statistics, such as the report by the National Congress of American Indians that states Native women are three times more likely to be sexually assaulted than white women.[3] Surely these concerns should also count as "real reservation issues."

An easy answer to the problems of inaccurate, insensitive, and harmful images might be to suggest that Native people themselves provide the visual representations of exoticness so desired in sports, cars, films, toys, and yes, Halloween costumes. Certainly tribes can and do manufacture and circulate self-exploitative images. The Mashantucket Pequot tribe's skimpy outfits for female casino employees have famously led to use of the term "Pocahoochies."

Yet, self-inscription in Native America is no less problematic than false representations by non-Indians. Take the current controversy that has developed as a result of the National Collegiate Athletic Association's resolution to ban disparaging Indian mascots from NCAA tournaments but allow Indian mascots for teams that receive permission from local tribes.[4] Certainly economic motivation has led to a lack of internal resolution about the appropriate use of "primitive" imagery. Rather than seek consistency of Native image production in a regulatory fashion, I'll strive in this essay to describe the contours of representational politics as they present themselves in particular contexts.

## Problems of Race

To talk about Indian art, you must talk about race. Indian arts demand an engagement with painful and, for some, confusing concepts, such as political sovereignty, indigenous legal rights, false representations, and histories of genocide. These very real manifestations of difference are premised on the articulation of racial difference. The difficulty of moving race to an overt categorization rather than a covert reference is the hesitancy to fully address the legacy of American conquest and domination.[5] Although the American public might prefer to be entertained by picturesque and docile Native nations or alternately shocked by the more exotic and brutal aspects of indigenous histories (as I write this, Mel Gibson's *Apocalypto* film is being released), it is clear at the turn of this new millennium that willful ignorance of, and complacency in, historically racist policies are all too evident to be ignored.

Part of the problem in understanding contemporary Indian arts is that the topic of race has been deemed an unacceptable variant to bring to the fore. Other ethnic artists can appear to leave the race question behind and move successfully into the mainstream. Consider curator Thelma Golden's famous declaration of "post-black," which managed to establish the whole field of contemporary African American and diasporic arts as open for serious contemplation.[6] A similar strategy has been attempted in Native American arts by individual artists such as Jimmie Durham, but it did not constitute a movement; there was no momentum behind his rejection of Native identity.[7]

While offering apparent freedom from constrictive categories imposed from the outside, a negation of ethnicity also implies a negation of history. This is the sense in which art historian Michael Harris asserts that "post-black" descriptives are problematic: "to suggest that race is no longer visualized, meaningful, or problematic seems incorrect and fanciful. The apparent danger is forgetful-ness of the power race exerts, even in the denial of its exis-tence."[8] In this manner, the "abandonment of an ethnic frame . . . mov[es] the artist into a frame that, by its seem-ing invisibility, closely resembles the way naturalized whiteness functions."[9]

The obvious key difference between Indian arts and the arts of any other perceived minority group in America is that "Native American" designates not only a racial / ethnic category but a sovereign political status as well. These potent attributes are not easily dismissed, cannot be easily dismissed. As author Eva Marie Garroutte re-minds her readers, there are real consequences in terms of loss of rights that accrue to Native American citizenship (often tied to "blood quantum"). She notes that "the ulti-mate and explicit federal intention was to use the blood quantum standard as a means to liquidate tribal lands and to eliminate government trust responsibility to tribes along with entitlement programs, treaty rights and reservations. Indians would eventually . . . become citizens indistinguish-able from all other citizens."[10] While artists of other ethnic backgrounds may find it beneficial to variously claim or reject identity constructs, the repercussions are greater for Native Americans in reference to access to rights and resources.

## Gender Dialogues

The addition of gender to discussions of race necessarily complicates the perceptions that the public has of Native American women and consequently the perceptions they have of themselves. Cherokee leader Wilma Mankiller's 2004 anthology, *Every Day Is a Good Day,* observes that the "appalling lack of accurate information about indigenous women fuels negative stereotypes. Television, film, and print media often portray indigenous women as asexual drudges or innocent children of nature," concluding that in the larger society, "the power, strength, and complexity of indigenous women are rarely acknowledged or recog-nized."[11] Native women's voices, then, add particularly important insights to notions of image politics not only as counternarratives to prevailing norms, but also as a reflec-tion of indigenous ideologies, such as communalism and politicization.

To claim identity beyond the princess / squaw, Native women artists create sites of knowledge production; they enact a cultured identity that embraces the communal, even as that act alienates them from trendy dialogues of fine-arts cultural hybridity. This procultural act ensures that Native women and their communities receive contin-ued acknowledgment as sovereign entities, eligible for recognition as indigenous nations, whereas individualis-tic or hybrid identity claims actually jeopardize this stand-ing. This female affiliation with the communal is why an indigenous knowledge systems approach is an appropriate interpretative tool for Native women's arts production.

Despite the prevailing acceptance of homogenized global sensibilities in media productions, many Native American and other indigenous artists continue to articu-late a sovereign, bounded, and discrete identity based on land, family, and memory. A continued sense of separate-ness, fully positioned in the unique status of tribal nations and their special relationship to the federal government, prevails. This boundedness, however, should not be inter-preted as static; belonging is not enforced but rather employed according to political, technical, economic, and educational developments and changes in the world at large. Both material and ideological constructs enable communal paradigms rather than individualistic or gen-dered identities to rise to the fore. As Nora Naranjo-Morse (Fig. 53) surmises, these strategic choices had everything to do with state practices of control and confinement:

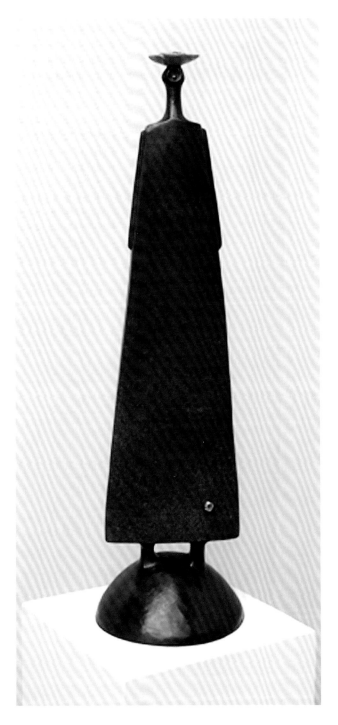

Fig. 53 *Thought Harvest, ED 10,* 2006
Nora Naranjo-Morse
Bronze, 35 × 9 × 9 in.

I think, the bottom line was, get these Indians to be a part of the mainstream. You know, we'll do what we need to do to get them to be dependent, to be consumers. And to be dependent on this structure. Because I think when you are farming, when you are building, you have to think. I mean, you have to think! You know? And the most dangerous thing is to think. To have women think? Oh god! To have children start thinking about how to build their own home, how to cultivate their own space, how to cultivate themselves. I think the people in the know who knew that the system we have was just an incredible organization because it was holistic. It encompassed religion. It encompassed the economy. It encompasses just everything. I think it works so well that it was very frightening. Why else would they come into the kivas and call us heathens and hit people and make us go underground with our ceremonies? Why were they killing us? Why were they redistributing the equal power in our communities that we had between the men and the women so that the men could then start governing and be more powerful than the women? There were reasons for all of that.

I think it's real easy now to get in your car and drive to Los Alamos and work as a secretary, and type someone else's letter. I'm not putting that down. I'm just saying that's what has happened for these people. That's where we're at now. That's the reality. But I think, it's easier to do that than to have to think, "Wait a minute, why did they do that?" Because then you start building installations that question it. Then you start saying, "Um, I don't know if I want to do that." Then you become a problem. And if it's only one person, OK. Oh my god, if you have lots of people then I think that gets a little troublesome.[12]

Fig. 54    *Rock Desert (Desert Rock),* 2007
Gloria Emerson
Acrylic and oil sticks on canvas, 36 × 24 in.

Naranjo-Morse's philosophical orientation as an artist may be read as an exercise in indigenous knowledge. Her decision, in her words, "to think"—to not be a consumer dependent on the structure of a capitalistic wage economy, but to engage in traditional behaviors of making structures (homes, installation art)—enacts indigenous knowledge systems. Making art is Naranjo-Morse's personal strategy for pursuing an anticolonial project. Problematically, this strategy of resistance is simultaneously defined by the U.S. capitalist economy within a web of economic constraints and opportunities.

Diné artist Gloria Emerson (Fig. 54) articulates her motivation as a producer of Native imagery as a personal and communal endeavor. If one looks closely at the articulation of self and community highlighted in Emerson's passage below, it is clear that she locates herself as an active agent within her society. Her decision to paint, while appearing to be beyond the borders of Navajo experience, is also a highly political act.

> I worked most of my life in social work, in education, administration, writing proposals, that sort of thing. And I always had been told by others that . . . the programs that I created or I administered were always creative and energetic, and so on. And I knew that somewhere along the way that I started to buy paints and canvas, and I started to work with clay and so on, but never formally trained, and it just started to grow on me during the '80s that I really had to do something for myself. Because everything that I had done was outwardly oriented. And I thought it was time for me. Time to turn inward, and to explore the inner world . . . not me, as an individual, but me as a phenomenon, me as a part of a tribe, and the changes we were going through. So, while I feel I am a case study, of what's going on

throughout the reservation, and I needed to get that out, and to document it in some way.[13]

Emerson's desire to capture and to convey her embrace of a tribal sensibility is clearly not an individualistic endeavor. She describes her artistic practice as an internal and personal one, yet this process is politically significant as well. She is, in her words, "a case study, of what's going on throughout the reservation."

The cultural values of gender and economics in the arts are both constitutive of, and reactive to, established paradigms of knowledge. These multiple sites of knowledge have the opportunity to be contested in the social arena of arts production and consumption, thereby allowing for highly charged articulations of identity claims. Qualities such as femaleness, maleness, isolation, belonging, and community find voice in these moments where conflicting ideologies meet.

I argue that if contemporary Indian arts are to be considered as a political manifestation of cultural identity, communal referents (tribal, pan-tribal, family) therefore take precedence over individual achievements (prestige, individual advancement). In this aspect and according to these frames of reference, the contemporary women artists interviewed exhibited an uncompromising allegiance to their extended lives as mothers, tradition-bearers, and wage earners.

## Realist Imagery—Representations Matter

My research, teaching, and activism stem from the premise that images are essential in constructing and conveying personhood. As image-makers, Native American artists struggle with the economic, cultural, and historical exploitation, erasure, and control of their cultural icons. Demeaning oral ("one little, two little"), visual (Land O'Lakes),

111

Fig. 55  *Woman in Stone,* 2006
Roxanne Swentzell
Stone, 8½ × 9 × 13½ in.

and dramatic (Chief Illiniwek mascot) expressions are ingrained American symbols that actively "work" to degrade and diminish personhood. This colonial legacy is often gendered, with the Native women as "alter" or other. As Michael Taussig relates, "In the visual scheme of things, it is not the men but the Indian women who are alter, and here everything pivots on releasing the spirit powers of appearance."[14]

Santa Clara artist Roxanne Swentzell (Fig. 55) relates how this formula works in practice:

> I remember one Indian market I got to my booth, it was still kind of dark and there were all these people there and I was still trying to wake up because it was still early. And I was preparing myself to open the door and get out and face all these people and, um,

and I had not put on my shoes yet because it was too early. So I decided I will just unload without my shoes so I don't trip. So I got out and I started unloading and then it became this thing that I was this barefoot sort of artist person. It fed into these people's ideas of who I am. In their mind [was] that I was so earthy or, so, and they really liked that. And maybe I am and I don't see that. But it wasn't done for an image, it was only [for a] practical reason. And if I . . . wanted to wear something fancy for instance and I showed up maybe in some heels or like that, I think people would be very upset that I'm not keeping to my image of what they have of me. And that's another box.[15]

Swentzell's narrative indicates a self-awareness of how her physical appearance supports ideas of cultural authenticity even as she diffuses its power by satire. Clearly the Indian princess / squaw, as demeaning and disturbing as this image often is, serves a deep-seated need in the American consciousness. Rayna Green attributes the prevalence of Indian stereotypes to the "xenophobic sociocultural framework into which they were channeled"[16] in American culture, noting the Indian woman "finds herself burdened with an image that can only be understood as dysfunctional."[17]

The "power of appearance" in contemporary Native imagery relates to Native women artists both as people and to the work they produce. The Indian woman embodies national ideologies, popular culture, and tribal identity in her person and her products. This double expectation, both that you be Indian in physical appearance and that your work conform to Indian art standards, could be argued to exist in equal strength both for Native men and women, but it is the women who bear the responsibility as communal artists more so than the men. They are more likely to be cast as the "cultural other."

While ignorance and racism may account for the persistence of the princess / squaw complex, I question the premise that more accurate data will necessarily lead to its demise. This optimistic view—that as public knowledge of Native American communities increases through more accurate and sensitive portrayals in the media, prejudice will diminish—is a mentalist reading based on attitude change alone, with no real material consequence attached. If one then watches a compelling film that confirms the plight of Native Americans as a virtuous one, a non-Indian viewer might feel more disposed to thinking twice about retelling a racist joke. He / she may even purchase a t-shirt or calendar with Native themes and feel progressive and tolerant.

Yet, how does this progressive ideal manifest itself when there are material consequences—economic development, rights to resources, even critiques of genocide? Most studies of stereotypes focus on the psychological harm inflicted upon the subject population; however iconic the ideals, the clusters of expectations surrounding Native women artists also have professional consequences that should not be overlooked. As social scientists Catherine Lutz and Jane Collins remind us, images are "never irrelevant, never unconnected to the world of actual social relations."[18]

## Pan-Indianism Reconsidered

It would seem easy enough to assign blame for racist typecasting to the power of seamless pan-Indian attributes. Devon Mihesuah states that "the two most prevalent images of Native women—the princess and the squaw drudge—still affect Native women's self-esteem."[19] Yet are these ideals monolithic? Or consistent over time? Scholars Jeffrey Hanson and Linda Rouse found that while stereotypes are "deeply embedded in American historical and contemporary consciousness," new pluralistic understandings of Indians may emerge alongside more traditional stereotypical paradigms of Indians.[20] Their findings proposed that demeaning stereotypes will be less prevalent in direct correlation to the diminishment of pan-tribal, homogeneous representations of Indians. In this scenario, non-Indians would be less likely to maintain negative Indian stereotypes if they were knowledgeable about a specific tribe, rather than just being exposed to pan-tribal, generic Indian references.

Their initial analysis proved false, however, for a subsequent study by the same researchers demonstrated that negative stereotyping continued as a result of status-based prejudice associated with competition over scarce resources, despite individual knowledge of particular tribes or people. In sum, a realist orientation prevailed because actual knowledge itself (a mentalist approach) did not alter negative appraisals when one ethnic or racial group was competing with another for social and economic resources. The controversy cited by the authors involved Chippewa treaty fishing rights in Wisconsin, where emotional anti-Indian sentiments were expressed by non-Indian commercial and sports fishermen. Negative personal stereotypes (Indians are lazy, lack ambition) were articulated in higher percentages in areas with greater Native American populations.[21] Status-based prejudice in this study is directly linked to resource allocation, not to monolithic ideas of identities. The mentalist approach—that a sensitive, fully informed America will relinquish legacies of hate and discrimination—does not apply when more realist concerns, such as access to material resources, are at play.

How does this sociological study inform our concern with art and images? Applied to the contemporary Indian arts world, mentalist codes work and prejudice is less evident when Native arts are exhibited by tribally specific designations and segregated from competition with other arts. Indian markets, traditionally known for the exhibition of tribally specific crafts, fit this definition of segregated contexts, for in these environments there is no competition with non-Indian artists. By contrast, when contemporary Indian arts enter the field of serious fine arts, competition for resources comes into play and racist practices (both covert and overt) emerge. Some examples may serve to illustrate how this formula works in practice.

The 2002 exhibition *Staging the Indian,* at the Tang Teaching Museum and Art Gallery at Skidmore College, featured the work of six contemporary Native American artists contrasted with historic photographs by Edward Curtis. Curtis is notable for his lifelong preoccupation with "capturing" the "vanishing" Indian. I exposed the problems inherent in this comparative methodology in a review of the exhibition in which I deemed this particular approach "re-active."[22] The exhibition methodology, however, was not the concern of *Daily Gazette* reviewer Carl Strock in his article titled "High Art and Low at the Tang."[23] It was the art itself and its presence in the college's "$10 million temple of culture in the center of campus"

that disturbed him. Calling the Native artists (Marcus Amerman, Judith Lowry, James Luna, Nora Naranjo-Morse, Shelley Niro, and Bently Spang) "alleged Native American artists—practitioners who clearly are, if nothing else, sophisticated enough to have insinuated themselves into the high-class art world of the white man," Strock then asserts "they have as much to do with American Indian culture as a beachball in China has to do with Chinese culture." Clearly, the exhibition breached key beliefs of who Indian artists are and where Indian art ought to belong.

Simultaneously, the segmentation of contemporary arts as distinct from the arts of any community has been labeled "an odd kind of segregational racism" by critics. The terms "ghettoize," "stereotyped," and "political," for example, were mobilized in critiques of the 1991 traveling exhibition *Our Land / Ourselves: American Indian Contemporary Artists,* curated by Flathead artist Jaune Quick-to-See Smith. Writing for Albany's *Times Union,* art reviewer Thomas Lail enacted the standard contradiction of both demanding the work look Indian, asking "Where's the culture?" while simultaneously decrying the premise of an exhibition that features only Native American art. He asserts: "The very idea of presenting an exhibit such as this is controversial since it works to segregate and ghettoize the works rather than present them as works on equal standing with other works."[24]

Both reviewers rejected the parameters of contemporary Native art exhibits on the basis of specific racial and fine arts mandates. While the *Staging the Indian* reviewer denied the authenticity of the exhibitors as Native and as artists, the *Our Land / Ourselves* reviewer demanded that the artists be both Natives and artists, defined as contradictions in terms. Both critiques deny the construct of pan-Indianism, or non-tribally specific arts safely exhibited as crafts. Clearly, the reviewers indicate, Native artists, if they are Native at all, must be distinct tribal representatives whose work conforms to historical norms. The allowance of multitribal referents, even the use of materials deemed not authentic, is enough to negate their ethnic and professional status. This approach enforces the either/or argument, whereby one may be one-dimensionally Native in ethnic reference and medium or not-Native in ethnic identification and medium. The common phrase "I'm an artist who happens to be Indian" does not in any way serve to question this false dichotomy, but rather strengthens the intolerant and oppressive intent of controlling Native identity in safe and nonthreatening ways.

The realist critique intersects significantly with pan-tribalism in the following ways. Realism in this instance references acceptance of modern engagement in urban and hybrid (read pan-Indian) environments where any artistic medium (film, as opposed to, say, basketry) may be adopted by Native artists. Mentalist codes argue that authenticity is linked only to tribally specific artists who work in non-modernist settings such as crafts fairs. Realism equates to pan-Indianism as a mentalist framework equates to traditional exhibition practices. It is far easier to assert that images have no real import, cannot cause damage, as the mentalist approach does, when the type of artwork referenced does not challenge established categories but stays safely in the crafts genre of tribal arts. Nativeness, in this schema, additionally signifies relinquishment of participation in individualizing environments, such as the fine arts world where tribalism has no place.

Clearly, notions of purity and containment are at play in these critiques, where clusters of attitudes that define "being Indian" are presented as unquestionable. Anthropologist Mary Douglas reminds us that concepts of purity and danger always involve symbolic systems. By defying standard categorization, contemporary Native artists take the form of matter out of place: "the by-product of a systematic ordering of classification of matter, in so far as ordering involves rejecting inappropriate elements."[25] The fine arts environment is acceptable in this perspective only if a Native artist becomes an individualist, a white man, thus maintaining the unspoken systematic classification. If artists present as both Indian and modern, they disrupt systems of reception as well as compete for scarce resources, thus activating racist stereotyping.

## The Right to Be Ethnic

One might productively ask, then, what is to be done? With such an imbalance in power to alter these controlling receptions of Indian art and identity, how does one begin to work toward a more humane understanding? For many scholars and activists, the answer has been to censor the ignorant visual and verbal depictions of Native Americans through either eradication or shame-based discourse. While these strategies may seem liberating in their intent, often the ignorance of wrong-headed thinking about Indian race politics continues, with demeaning commentaries safely operating in a segregated fashion in a covert manner. I argue that the enduring nature of stereotypes indicates that essentialized images are vital in the interaction of diverse groups. The tendency for this essentialization to be viewed in primarily negative terms, as the majority of the literature on stereotypes does, inhibits alternative interpretations of its use.

Pan-tribal or essentialized images are not the culprit of social oppression—in fact it is the "every Indian" image that often provides the opportunity for a political critique of demeaning typecasting. Imagery and ideas do exert pressure on exoticized others and should be considered as real constraints, yet they can also be enabling. The existence and use of broad generalized categories of reference in itself is not inherently damaging and can be usefully mobilized in inter- and intragroup dynamics. Hanson and

Fig. 56    *Some Kind of Buckaroo,* 1990
Jean LaMarr
Serigraph, 24 × 36 in.

Rouse's assertion that "differences between ethnic groups
... can be accented and/or exaggerated by racial and ethnic
stereotypes" makes sense in this analysis only if we also
consider the additional possibility that these differences, as
expressed by stereotypes, also have other potentials, including self-inscription, political mobilization, and the enhance-
ment of communication between disparate groups.[26]

For example, consider the following comment by Pit
River Paiute artist Jean LaMarr (Fig. 56) as she critiques
the difference she perceives in art-making values:

> Well, I don't think monetary achievement is my
> ultimate goal, even though I would like to feel com-
> fortable. I hear a lot of Indian artists [say], "I want
> to be rich, and I want to be the R. C. Gorman, or
> the Fritz Scholder, or the ultimate." To me that's

almost a White man's philosophy, or a White man's
artist goal.[27]

LaMarr's ability to articulate what she perceives as a
proper way of approaching the arts in a Native context is
dependent on comparison with white man's behavior for
economic gain alone. The dismissed categorization of white
man mobilizes the positive categorization of what Indian
artists should strive for—community responsibility and
mentorship. In this instance, Indians who act like white
men are suspect.

Discussions of what constitutes a breach in proper
behavior in the arts are often animated by the offensive
Native images produced by non-Indians, as in artist Laura
Fragua's narrative:

> I saw this Hopi, this sculpture of a maiden with a
> butterfly whorl. And that's a maiden, that's a young
> girl. She's a virgin. And they had this ... this sculp-
> ture was this woman, but she must have had a bust-
> ier on and it pushed her boobs up and she had this

big old cleft and her manta came down and it was slit down to the middle. Hopi maiden! That's a maiden! It doesn't look like a maiden to me!

You have to know what, because you are a part of that culture, you know what the dos and don'ts [are]. And because the people who did the artwork depict Indian people doing things, they've got it all wrong.[28]

The articulation of Pueblo values in this example is enacted in response to the faulty ideas of others. This oppressive imagery, as hurtful and clearly wrong as it is, has triggered a conversation about what is acceptable in the Pueblo community (the dos and don'ts), what codes a Native reading might reveal (the whorl signifies virginity), and the expression of a political position (wrongness). Each of these values is effectively communicated via false images—stereotypes. Theorist Richard Handler argues that

groups do not have essential identities; indeed, they ought not to be defined as things at all. For any imaginable social group—defined in terms of nationality, class, locality, or gender—there is no definitive way to specify "who we are," for "who we are" is a *communicative process* [my emphasis] that includes many voices and varying degrees of understanding and, importantly, misunderstanding.[29]

Likewise, Linda Martin Alcoff states that the critique of identity (its "negative valence") as essentializing has "failed to answer the challenge posed by accounts that understand identity as a *process* [my emphasis] of meaning making."[30]

This communicative process is a key consideration for how Native women grapple with the imposed identity references of others and thus form new self-referents in response. Instead of rejecting or eliminating the false

stereotypes of squaw or princess, human actors can and do fashion new referents, positioning themselves in unique, complex, and layered selves that draw from, but are not fully inhibited by, the imposing ignorance of otherness. This reworking is indicative of creative adaptations and key response methods for grappling with the impact of Westernization and as such should be considered as an essential component of indigenous knowledge systems at play.

## Binaries and Alterity

I advance a theory that claims that the "othering" in identity politics, stereotypes, and role referents can be an essential component of self-inscription. This processual view of identity does not claim to explain identity formation but sheds light on the communicative aspect of identity. It is in this communicative function that we conceptualize our varied positions, our conceptions of reality. In the words of Satya P. Mohanty, "our identities are ways of making sense of our experiences. Identities are theoretical constructions that enable us to read the world in specific ways."[31]

I have found it useful in my work on stereotypes to reference the twin concepts of binaries and alterity. Simply stated, binaries are the conceptual categories that are used to delineate self from others. Binaries are like fences between neighbors: my property ends here, yours begins there. Binaries require segmentation, a dichotomous reading of selfhood that in itself does not indicate an oppressive agency. Like fences, dichotomies exist as inert terms that are not to be willfully interpreted as polarized arguments.[32] This is the manner in which I read stereotypes, as communicative devices of expressing boundaries.

Similarly, alterity connotes "the mode of division of a field."[33] When Native artists refer to "white man thinking" or when collectors refer to Indian aesthetics, a compare-and-contrast ideology is often enacted. A white man is

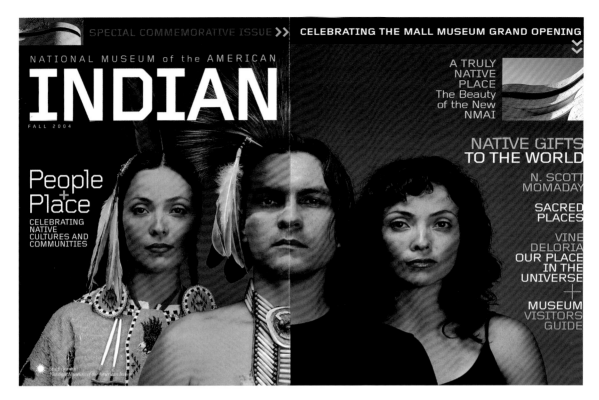

118

Fig. 57     Cover, *National Museum of the American Indian* magazine, fall 2004

what an Indian is not, Indian art is something that non-ethnically specific art is not. Alterity has been described by Ernest van Alphen as a "screen for the imagination," a "code," and "a device of meaning-production":

> The only way to know the other is by letting the other speak about me, by giving the other the position of "I." When "I" speak about the other, I remain in fact caught in the process of defining or demarcating my self-image. The other is used as a screen on which ideals or terrors can be projected, or as locations to which problematic feelings about self can be displaced.[34]

How is the theory of alterity manifest in Native communities? Robert Berkhofer's 1979 analysis, *The White Man's Indian,* demonstrates that white images of Indians tell more about white attitudes and perceptions than elucidating any realities of Indian life. In this "paradigm of polarity," whites assume uniqueness as classifiers and

Native Americans as classified only through the content of specific imagery that persists over time, "since Whites primarily understood the Indian as antithesis to themselves, then civilization and Indianness as they defined them would forever be opposites."[35]

Alterity is perhaps *the* central organizing principle in assessing Native American imagery. A close reading of the inaugural magazine cover for the National Museum of the American Indian (Fig. 57) evidences the construction of binaries at play, suggesting potent codes of reference. The exterior cover of this commemorative 2004 issue depicts a direct reference to conforming ideals about Indianness. The Native man appears in the foreground bare-chested and, like the fully clothed Native woman in the background, facing the camera. Obvious interpretations of the woman as subservient and of the man as virile may be made, but we will focus our analysis on the gaze of the subjects toward the viewer.

While a frontal pose utilizing eye contact may seem to signify a desire or availability for communication across the printed page, visual theorists suggest the opposite—to look out at the viewer represents the accessibility of the "other" depicted. The head-on camera gaze suggests

Fig. 58    *Angel DeCora on steps of College Hall,*
           *Smith College,* n.d.
           4¾ × 3¾ in.

Fig. 59    *Angel DeCora in native dress,* n.d.
           Photographic print, tinted brown, 6½ × 4¼ in.

documentary aims and is more often associated with scientific inquiries and criminal documentation than portraiture. Scholars Lutz and Collins note that "those who are culturally defined as weak—woman, children, people of color, the poor, the tribal rather than the modern, those without technology—are more likely to face the camera, the more powerful to be represented looking elsewhere."[36]

Once the reader fully opens the magazine, an inner cover appears, depicting the same Native man and woman in Western dress. The Native woman remains behind the man, but in this pose, she is the bare one of the two, her loose, shoulder-length hair suggestively grazing a form-fitting tank top. What codes are read in this set of images? Clearly the Native woman depicts the princess (outside cover) and squaw (inside cover); the man the warrior (outside cover) and the buck (inside cover). It is certain that the National Museum of the American Indian intended a positive reading of Native Americans as real people, just like

you and me, even though they do wear traditional outfits at powwows and museum openings. This universalist intent draws directly on the binary of Native/non-Native, other/one-of-us. Through the use of alterity, readers may project themselves upon the Native subjects of the inside cover—"this could be me, it could be my friend"—while the outside, public cover calls attention to the exotic nature of Indianness that cannot be easily adopted by any reader. The direct eye contact may appear to invite readings of accessibility and communication, but it also signals the possibility of ownership: a nonthreatening otherness that may be safely possessed.

The use of what is commonly termed the "contrast picture" is indicative of the binary references "primitive" and "civilized." Note that there are only two worlds in this equation—no complicating examples of hybridity spoil the clear reading available to the viewer. This constructed image visually represents the decades-long work to establish, organize, fund, build, and administer the first national museum of its kind devoted to living Native peoples of North and South America. As the central visual code of reference, this key image draws directly upon existing stereotypes as the most effective communicative device for reaching its audience. Why is this equation of alterity so pervasive, so consistent?

Scholar Edward Spicer states that the formation and maintenance of persistent identity systems is "intimately bound up with the conditions of opposition," adding "it appears that the oppositional process is the essential factor in the formation and development of the persistent identity system."[37]

I wish to juxtapose for a moment the photographs on page 119 as a testimony to the malleability and historicism of the contrast-picture technique. These photographs are of Angel DeCora, a Winnebago woman who attended Smith College in Northampton, Massachusetts, from 1892 to 1896. DeCora's life achievements were substantial—after Smith, she studied at Drexel Institute and the Boston Museum of Fine Arts School, worked professionally in New York and Boston as a commercial illustrator, taught at Carlisle Indian School, and lectured internationally on Native arts at conferences held by the International Congress of Americanists, the National Education Association, and the Society of American Indians. In 1919, DeCora died of pneumonia in Northampton, where she was buried in an unmarked grave.

The image politics evidenced in DeCora's portraits (Figs. 58 and 59), taken some hundred years earlier than the NMAI cover, reflect as well the contrast of civilized and exotic other, but note here, importantly, that DeCora's gaze is averted from the camera; she makes no eye contact with the lens. Additionally her whole body is captured for the viewer, not a segmented body as in the NMAI photo set. The photographs of DeCora provide a context—the halls

of academia and the great outdoors—as contrasted with the solid gray backdrop of the Smithsonian photos. In both images DeCora is fully clothed and is not in apparent need of a male guardian. I suggest that DeCora's historic representations imply a more progressive political reading than the 2004 Smithsonian pairing.

Given the vastly different political climate of the early twentieth century, how do we account for the seemingly empowered stance, the privilege of looking away from the camera, the dignity of the clothing and hair? These very different sets of contrast pictures imply that the principles of realism, pan-Indianism, and stereotypes may be productively mobilized as inert communicative devices, free from overly oppressive readings suggested by the codes of analysis commonly tied to stereotypes. Their absolute free-floating availability as signifiers of vastly different times, places, and intended meanings indicates their malleability as well as their utility in conveying personhood and power (or lack of it).

## Embrace the Stereotype

An alternative reading of the Indian stereotype calls for new analyses whereby the depiction of common imagery inspires productive actions. It is crucial that this freedom to interrogate icons of Indianness remains uncensored, for as I have argued, to do otherwise would inhibit the process of communicating and therefore understanding identity. A central aspect of detangling the collapsing of codes inherent in stereotyping is to understand how ethnic identities are conceptualized by Native American artists. How are the arts conceptualized by the producers themselves? What types of criticisms are useful for their practice?

While it is clear that contemporary Native arts today cannot be defined under the category of ethnographic or tribal arts, the field has still not reached the critical

Fig. 60    *Suite: INDIAN, Mars Thundercloud Gets a Calling,* 2002
          Shelley Niro
          Video still

assessment of fine arts museums and galleries. This is due, I think, to assumptions about the primacy of communal norms that are more likely to be expressed using terms such as "identity" or "culture"—descriptives that are not specific only to "small-scale" societies but could also be applied to any social unit—and to notions of timelessness. Native artists who move in both mainstream fine arts and rural reservation communities defy the dated analysis that strictly sees the tribal as separate in time and space from the modern.[38]

The concept of Native Americans as mobile, contemporary, and, simultaneously, tribal has not yet been recognized by the non-Indian public. Although most Native artists would not inherently see themselves as insurmountably grappling with two foreign cultures—one traditional, one modern—their lives are still patterned and restricted by the ethnic qualifier "Indian" and the misconceptions of those unfamiliar with contemporary Native cultures. Do

these perceptions of others lead to self-inscription? More specifically, does the act of addressing these misconceptions fuel identity? If so, can even negative referents advance positive self-representation?

Images matter to these conversations because visual literacy is tied to cultural competency. Both the motivation to alter preconceived notions of the Native as well as the availability of counternarratives are strikingly missing from general discourse, yes. But the solution to a greater literacy in Native arts is not found in the kind or amount of information available. Elimination of derogatory stereotypes and an increase in more accurate media representations have been unquestionably understood as the standard cure for American ignorance. The resiliency of stereotyped images demonstrates that eradication alone is not an available or effective option.[39] An upsurge of more sensitive portrayals in print and media might allow for an altered stereotype, but stereotypes will still be employed, negating the substantial shifts in perception desired.

What must be accomplished, and what I think artists are trying to accomplish, is the engagement of flawed images as a means of capturing their power for alternate

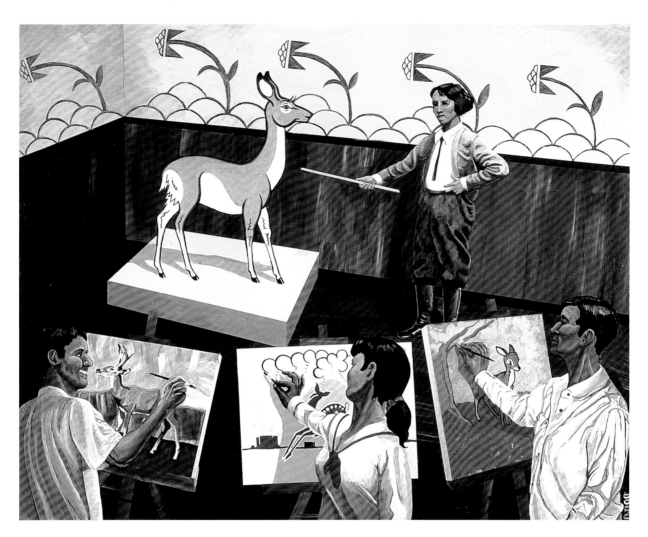

Fig. 61    *Bambi Makes Some Extra Bucks at the Studio,* 2002
America Meredith
Acrylic on Masonite, 26½ × 32½ in.

readings. Until the utility of "institutionalized icons"[40] is dissected, their potency will remain high, and their circulation will certainly remain in place in mainstream culture.

An example of how iconic Native imaging is incorporated proactively can be found in the work of Shelley Niro. Her film *Mars Thundercloud Gets a Calling* (featured in the compilation *Suite: INDIAN*) (Fig. 60) depicts a young Native woman eagerly consuming all manner of Native identifiers, from posters, books, and beadwork to princess pageants.[41] The character's desperateness to be Indian is conveyed in a poignant and ironic manner. The effect is startling—aren't only non-Indians supposed to be doing this crazy wannabe stuff? By allowing an identifiably Native woman to harbor the same doubts and resort to the same signifiers of feathers and fans that the non-Indian audience can imagine themselves doing, Niro breaks loose the precious safeguarding of tradition and allows for creative play about outward signifiers of identity. Niro's work successfully conveys the inner doubts, ramblings, and everydayness of contemporary identity by embracing some pretty disturbing and everyday notions, such as Native people as craftsmen, Native people as homeless, Native people as entertainers. She takes the audience to its intended place of arrival and then takes it beyond that.

Another image that is useful to contemplate in reference to ironic adaptation of historic and limiting icons is America Meredith's 2002 *Bambi Makes Some Extra Bucks at the Studio* (Fig. 61). The centerpiece of the work is a brilliant blue deer and his companion, a stern-looking female arts instructor who points at him with a lecturer's stick, hand on hip, while diligent Indian art students work steadily at their canvases. The "gotcha" aspect of the work is its deliberately sarcastic reference to the Santa Fe Indian School's genre of arts instruction, known alternately as the Dorothy Dunn School (named after its legendary instructor) or (derogatorily) the Bambi School of Painting for its

flat, two-dimensional design-saturated style.[42] Meredith brings the blue Bambi to life for us to consume, contemplate, and laugh about, even though the 1930s Indian School arts instruction is known to be coercive and controlling. If one were unable to render the blue Bambi, a critique would likewise not be possible.

While these reappropriations may be interpreted as reifying dichotomies of the individual and the collective, I suggest that their performances serve as a means of owning, controlling, and redirecting existing interpretative frameworks for subjective alternative ends.

The Indian art world demands more of the viewer than aesthetic contemplation alone. To fully engage in Indian arts, one must participate in a fairly rigorous intellectual exercise in which personal doubt may productively serve to further one's depth of understanding. Counterintuitive measures such as an embrace of stereotypes, generic Indian identity, and realism are reasonable places to start the difficult process ahead.

## Notes

1. Robert Bieder, "Anthropology and History of the American Indian," *American Quarterly* 33, no. 3 (1981): 309–26.

2. Ron Toya, "Free Speech: Another Side of the 'Redskin' Debate." Posted: August 31, 2006, www.indiancountry .com.

3. National Congress of American Indians. Undated fact sheet, "Violence against Indian Women in Indian Country," http://www.ncai.org/ncai/ advocacy/hr/docs/dv-fact_sheet.pdf. Last accessed 2/11/08.

4. "NCAA Executive Committee Issues Guidelines for Use of Native American Mascots at Championship Events," http://www.ncaa.org/wps/ portal/!ut/p/kcxml/04_Sj9SPykssy 0xPLMnMz0vM0Y_QjzKLN4j3NQ DJgFjGpvqRqCKO6AI-YXA RX4_83FSgeKQ5kG_k7akfoh_pou-t H6BfkBsaGlFuaOHoqKgIANUmV EM!/delta/base64xml/L3dJdyEvd0ZN QUFzQUMvNElVRS82XzBfTFU!?CO NTENT_URL=http://www2.ncaa.org/ portal/media_and_events/press_ room/2005/august/20050805_exec_ comm_rls.html. Last accessed 12/07/07.

5. Faye Harrison, "Unraveling Race for the Twenty-First Century," in *Exotic No More: Anthropology on the Frontlines,* ed. Jeremy MacClancy (Chicago: University of Chicago Press, 2002), 145–66.

6. Onajide Shabaka, "National Black Arts Festival All in a Name?" *Miami Art Exchange,* July 22, 2005. http://www .miamiartexchange.com/miami_art_ articles/miami_art_articles_2005/ national_black_arts_festival_all_in_a_ name.html. Last accessed 12/07/07.

7. Laura Turney, "Ceci n'est pas Jimmie Durham," *Critique of Anthropology* 19, no. 4 (1999): 423–42.

8. Michael Harris, *Colored Pictures: Race and Visual Representation* (Chapel Hill: University of North Carolina Press, 2003), 257.

9. Ibid., 248–49.

10. Eva Marie Garroutte, "The Racial Formation of American Indians: Negotiating Legitimate Identities within Tribal and Federal Law," *American Indian Quarterly* 25, no. 2 (2001): 224–39.

11. Wilma Mankiller, *Every Day Is a Good Day: Reflections by Contemporary Indigenous Women* (Golden, CO: Fulcrum, 2004), 8.

12. Nora Naranjo-Morse, interview with author, August 11, 1997.

13. Gloria Emerson, interview with author, 1991.

14. Michael Taussig, *Mimesis and Alterity: A Particular History of the Senses* (New York: Routledge, 1993), 129.

15. Roxanne Swentzell, interview with author, September 12, 2000.

16. Rayna Green, "The Indian in Popular American Culture," in *Handbook of North American Indians,* ed. William C. Sturtevant, vol. 4, *History of Indian-White Relations* (Washington, DC: Smithsonian Institution Press, 1988), 587–606.

17. Rayna Green, "The Pocahontas Perplex," in *Unequal Sisters: A Multicultural Reader in U.S. Women's History,* ed. Ellen Carol DuBois and Vicki L. Ruiz (New York: Routledge, 1990), 17.

18. Catherine Lutz and Jane Collins. *Reading National Geographic* (Chicago: University of Chicago Press, 1993), 3.

19. Devon A. Mihesuah, *Indigenous American Women* (Lincoln: University of Nebraska Press, 2003), 102.

20. Jeffrey R. Hanson and Linda P. Rouse, "Dimensions of Native American Stereotyping," *American Indian Culture and Research Journal* 11, no. 4 (1987): 34.

21. Jeffrey R. Hanson and Linda P. Rouse, "American Indian Stereotyping, Resource Competition, and Status-based Prejudice," *American Indian Culture and Research Journal* 15, no. 3 (1991): 1–17.

22. Nancy Mithlo, review of *Staging the Indian: The Politics of Representation,* in *American Anthropologist* 105, no. 1 (March 2003), 156–61.

23. Carl Strock, "High Art and Low at the Tang," *Schenectady (NY) Daily Gazette,* February 21, 2002.

24. Thomas Lail, "Exhibit Takes Very Few Risks," *Albany Times Union,* March 14, 1991.

25. Mary Douglas, *Purity and Danger: An Analysis of Concepts of Pollution and Taboo* (London: Ark Paperbacks, 1966), 35.

26. Hanson and Rouse, "American Indian Stereotyping, Resource Competition, and Status-based Prejudice," 2.

27. Jean LaMarr, interview with author, 1991.

28. Laura Fragua, interview with author, 1991.

29. Richard Handler, "Is 'Identity' a Useful Concept?" in *Commemorations: The Politics of National Identity,* ed. John R. Gillis (Princeton, NJ: Princeton University Press, 1994), 27–40, 30.

30. Linda Martin Alcoff, "Who's Afraid of Identity Politics?" in *Reclaiming Identity: Realist Theory and the Predicament of Postmodernism,* ed. Paula M. L. Moya and Michael R. Hames-Garcia (Berkeley: University of California Press, 2000), 325.

31. Satya P. Mohanty, "The Epistemic Status of Cultural Identity," in *Reclaiming Identity: Realist Theory and the Predicament of Postmodernism,* 43.

32. Val Plumwood, "Feminism and the Logic of Alterity," in *Representing Reason: Feminist Theory and Formal Logic,* ed. Rachel Joffe Falmagne and Majorie Hass (New York: Rowman & Littlefield, 2002), 45–70.

33. Ibid.

34. Ernest van Alphen, "The Other Within," in *Alterity, Identity, Image: Selves and Others in Society and Scholarship,* ed. Raymond Corbey and Joep Leerssen (Atlanta: Rodopi Press, 1991), 1–16, 15.

35. Robert F. Berkhofer Jr., *The White Man's Indian: Images of the American Indian from Columbus to the Present* (New York: Vintage Books, 1979), 29.

36. Lutz and Collins, *Reading National Geographic,* 199.

37. Edward H. Spicer, "Persistent Cultural Systems," *Science* 174, no. 4011 (1971): 795–800, 797.

38. Philip Deloria, *Indians in Unexpected Places* (Lawrence: University Press of Kansas, 2004).

39. Mark R. Connolly, "What's in a Name? A Historical Look at Native American–Related Nicknames and Symbols at Three U.S. Universities," *Journal of Higher Education* 71, no. 5 (2000): 515–47.

40. C. Richard King, "Bad Anthropologies: Scholars, Sports Fans, and Native American Mascots," *InterCulture* (Florida State University Dept. of Interdisciplinary Humanities) 2, no. 1 (2005), http://iph.fsu.edu/interculture. Last accessed 12/07/07.

41. Shelley Niro, *Suite: INDIAN.* Videotape, 2005, distributed by Vtape, Toronto.

42. Laurie Eldridge, "Dorothy Dunn and the Art Education of Native Americans: Continuing the Dialogue," *Studies in Art Education* 42, no. 4 (2001): 318–32.

*The Discoverer,* 1991
Bob Haozous
Paint on steel, 17 × 6 × 3 ft.

## CHAPTER 5

Métis Loretta Todd tells a story of a nineteenth-century European painter "recording" Native people on the Great Plains: "While he was painting a Native man on a horse, another Native man observed the artist's work and remarked how his painting was wrong" because he showed only one leg of the rider and two of the horse. "The Native man reminded the artist that the horse had four legs and the rider two, which should all be shown."[1]

This is not a story about primitive naiveté but about the ways Western culture forces Native people to stay partly invisible. Is there a way to show all the legs and ride away on them? Or is indigenous America still "outside representation," as Alfred Young Man wrote in an uncompromising essay for the *Indigena* catalog in 1992?[2] In another sense, Jean Fisher describes the "faultline" between what she calls "the ungraspable real"—the cultural differences that remain illegible to white people—and "the imaginary sign (. . . which Indian peoples themselves are under pressure to accept as real)."[3] Or in yet another way of thinking about this problem, by turning it back on itself: "If the Other has no form, the One ceases to exist," as African scholar Olu Oguibe writes, intriguingly making non-Indian America dependent for its very existence on correct perceptions of Native people.[4]

At the time, Young Man was searching for "the Native perspective"—a new frame of reference for scholarly analysis and criticism of Native art—believing that "Native American self determination lives on through art." Apache Bob Haozous's 2005 show in Santa Fe vehemently advocated for Indian art that talks to Indian people, even as he acknowledges "the white man in all of us." He asks for an internal dialogue that doesn't so much exclude non-Indians as it justifiably disregards us and our needs, bypassing "Indian modernism," "cultural prettiness," and "two worlds." An unabashed political artist, Haozous throws down the gauntlet to his peers when he says, "I don't think there are any

## All Six Legs
*by Lucy R. Lippard*

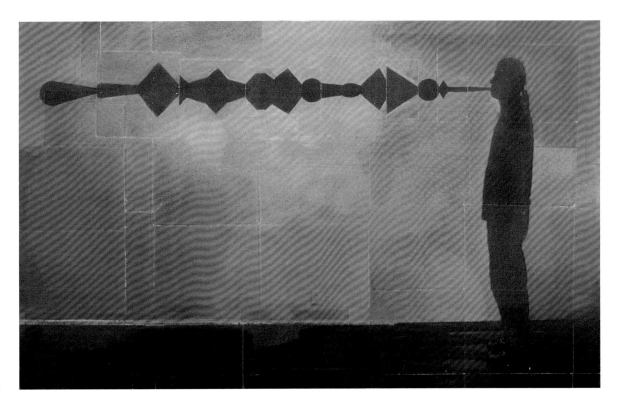

*Exhale,* 1998
Kimowan McLain
Mixed media, 36 × 54 in.

Indian artists making important contemporary Indian art
... because we don't have a cultural language to speak from."[5]

Is Young Man's "Native perspective" or Haozous's
"cultural language" even available to non-Indians? If it
were, would that just constitute another colonial appropriation? (Sometimes being white and writing sympatheti-
cally about artists of color, you feel you're damned if you
do, and damned if you don't, and the only way to continue
is to be willing to have your foot in your mouth half the
time.) Anyway I'm still trying to figure out if non-Indian
critics and curators are part of the problem or just part of
the equation. One of the best statements by an artist on the
role of the critic is what an anonymous friend told curator
and writer Bruce Bernstein: "Keep talking while we keep
working, but hold it down so I can hear myself think."[6]

At the same time, the evil twins—assimilation and
appropriation—travel both ways. Instead of pursuing a
deeper and unfamiliar knowledge, non-Indian writers tend
to depend on our own culturally approved taste, education,
and background, which is rooted in Western civilization,
no matter how rebellious and sympathetic to the non-
Western we think we are. Native writers who have that
knowledge are in turn sometimes overdependent on Western theory instead of swallowing it with a grain of salt. We
share a liminal place, not entirely sure of what our roles
should be.

The notion of *liminality* comes from the Latin word
for threshold, or the initial stage of a process. Activity is
implied, along with some hesitation. The threshold leads
somewhere—inside or outside; it is neither a stopping
point, nor a waiting room. Those who have stepped over
the threshold have entered a different space. All contemporary Indian artists are aware of the delicate line they must
tread between honoring their traditions and at the same
time making their own art distinguishable from that of
others, as demanded by the mainstream avant garde. The
vaunted "originality" that sustained modernism for so
many decades has since given way to the splintered virtues
of postmodernism, which can actually favor the witty and
recalcitrant inventiveness of Native artists. From this point
of view, you would have to look for the missing legs of
horse and rider somewhere else in the picture.

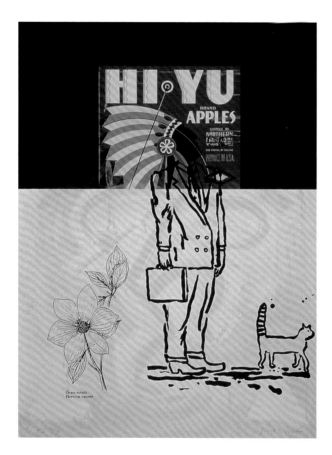

*Modern Times,* 1993
Jaune Quick-to-See Smith
Lithograph, 30 × 22 in.

The concepts of hybridity, transcultural spaces, strategic essentialism, and other new ways of getting around the classic Eurocentricity of the modernist art world have opened up new cross-cultural negotiations, with parallel models in African, Asian, and Latin countries. Intermarriage and other life choices have allowed many artists an array of "identities" with which to confound those who want to keep them in their place.

Younger Native artists and writers acknowledge that indigeneity is an ideological space that can be worked in, and on. Aware that no single person, style, or subject can possibly "represent" Native America, they can reject the reduction of Native art to a simplistic spectacle of difference. Apache Nancy Mithlo describes her own generation of Native writers as

> thirty somethings who have enough confidence and training to openly question the mandates of an over-zealous market, but who find ourselves on a short rope when it comes to exposing the naiveté of our patrons lest we find ourselves abandoned by the only transportation left. Too old to be overly optimistic, too young to be crassly cynical, we tread boldly into uncharted territory without the protection that age may afford and lacking a certain stupidity that may have been charming ten years earlier.[7]

Oscar Howe kicked open the doors in 1958 with his famous statement on being rejected from the Philbrook Museum of Art's Annual because his work was too modernist to be "Indian": "Who ever said that my paintings are not in traditional Indian style has poor knowledge of Indian art indeed. There is much more to Indian art than pretty, stylized pictures."[8] He and others pointed out that the origins of their formal experiments were not in Western modernism but came from within their own "art histories," despite the fact that indigenous people have long

*Transmitter to the Gods,* 2004
Da-ka-xeen Mehner
Photograph, 24 × 20 in.

*Most Serene Republics: HONOR MORTE DI NUMSHIM*
*"SHOW INDIANS" RAMMENTARE,* 2007
Edgar Heap of Birds
Mylar on steel panel, 24 × 36 in.

been denied both "art" and "history," except those so designated by the dominant culture. It *is* history, whether or not it's written down by white people. Mi'Kmaq video artist Mike MacDonald quotes an elder who said that "the great crime in this land was not that the natives had their language and culture beaten out of them in boarding schools—the great crime was that the people who came here did not adopt the culture of the land."[9]

Among the challenges facing Native artists today is figuring out where the line should be drawn between an indigenous artist making modernist or postmodernist art and a modernist/postmodernist artmaker who "happens to be indigenous." Modernism and tradition are sometimes presented as incompatible, like art and politics, oil and water. Yet for many Native artists, tradition is not the antithesis of modernism, but its mulch. The identification of all modernism with Western art history has held some as rebels in their traditional ways, refusing to trade in

their culture for assimilation, holding out for "aesthetic sovereignty." On the other hand, the "traditional" (or the neo-traditional) has so often become so romanticized and trivialized that some Native artists have refused to make anything recognizable as "Indian art," and some of them take refuge in the purported "universality" of high art. Commercial motives have inexorably played their part; "Indian art," so influenced by traders and external interpretation, is well defined in the minds of buyers looking for the "authentic" (and often falling for the inauthentic). Ghettoization preoccupies every identity-based or marginalized group. But it too is double-sided. While most Indian artists would like to be shown in broader contexts, I doubt if many want to see the end of Native art exhibitions. In the early days of the feminist movement we were constantly put down for demanding women's shows, as though we hadn't been going to *men's* shows most of our lives. A decade later, identity politics began to be dismissed

Fig. 62   *Real Indians*, 1977
Larry McNeil
Silver gelatin photograph, 24 × 24 in.

in academic circles as "essentialist." But there wouldn't have been any deconstruction without a construction (and I don't mean a construct)—something to build on and tear down and build on again. Let's face it, if a woman artist makes a big reputation under a male name or Native artists never mention their tribal affiliations, nothing is gained for the constituencies we care most about. All artists need to be full participants in the larger society. I'm reminded of Ad Reinhardt, the Lithuanian American known for his apparently solid-black paintings; he was a political socialist and activist but kept all that strictly out of his art, because, as he said, "Art is art and everything else is everything else." The message is that if racism bothers you and it won't fit into your art, go out and do something else about it.

There is a certain built-in element of activism in the very process of making Native art because for so many, community remains an important element even when the work doesn't fall into the external category of "community arts" (e.g., murals, gardens, children's projects, etc.), and even when an artist's work may converge with the mainstream more and less often at times in her or his life. Contemporary artists continue to try to make art that will "read" both in their own communities and outside, while maintaining aesthetic independence. There's always a push and pull between those artists who have gone out into the world but also want to communicate with those at home, and those traditionalists who often see newly acquired Western egos as taking energy and talent away from the community and change as a threat to already threatened artistic customs playing an important role in some tribal economies. Yet Native societies have generally honored creativity and change. Eventually, pride in their artists' successes seems to replace fear of exploitation.

Comanche writer Paul Chaat Smith names the place where Native artists work today: "A space carved from

hard lessons and bitter disappointment, a ruthless ambition for intellectual integrity and rejection of tired rhetoric, a passionate belief that our endlessly surprising communities are capable of anything, and a willingness to laugh, especially at the latest regulations from the Indian thought police."[10] Contemporary Native artists also have a lot of options. They can reject the aesthetic autonomy of modernism, its conventional separation from politics, activism, and real life. They can choose to make work that is not discernibly "Indian," while maintaining the context in which they make art; in that context lies their allegiance to their home places and peoples. Several well-known artists live or spend time on their reservations, participating in daily cultural and ceremonial life there as well as in the white world where their art is, ironically, sometimes better received than it is on the reservation. Some become mediators, or "translator's children," to paraphrase what writer Joseph Bruchac has called mixed bloods.

Although it is often assumed that those who have been dislocated from their homelands are at a disadvantage, some of the most interesting art being made today is by those who are fully conscious of their physical separation from homelands as a modern condition. Larry McNeil, for instance, has offered himself up in his art as a "Real Indian" (Fig. 62), spoofing the American thirst for "authenticity" while simultaneously showing pride in his Tlingit identity and emphasizing place as a crucial component in his art. Although the periphery may not always be a comfortable place, it is potentially a highly creative place. Gerald McMaster calls this area between reservation and urban communities "Reservation X"—

a socially ambiguous zone, a site of articulation for the aboriginal contemporary artist that is frequently crossed, experienced, interrogated, and negotiated. This idea argues for a space of radical openness and

134

*Certificate of Indian Blood,* 1993
Melanie Yazzie
Cyanotype and screenprint, 22 × 15 in.

*Reclamation,* 1994–99
Kay Miller
Oil, mirrors, and rhinestones, 60 × 48 in.

'hybridity,' or spaces of resistance being opened at the margins. I, however, see this space as in between two centers, which is a politically charged, though highly permeable, site.[11]

Kiowa/Italian American Keri Ataumbi says that her "gripe about Native American art is there's so much nostalgia wrapped up in it . . . The trick is to keep it vibrant."[12] She works in one of the great liminal places—the zone of unselfconscious denial of divisions between so-called fine art and so-called crafts or applied arts, which offers a number of new directions simply by ignoring the Western tabus set up by centuries of differentiation. Her Lucite-and-cast-iron table (Fig. 63) is a Native version of the Chinese saying "women hold up half the sky." Like the huge, plain white apron that was shown above it, the table is oversized and about strength. It is held up by casts of the artist's own arms—a reference to the social role of women and the strength it takes to nourish a culture. Ataumbi had to work out for months to get muscular enough to "hold up" this monumental table. Her jewelry, or wearable art, she says, also addresses the relationship between object and the body—a longtime preoccupation of feminist artists as well as a confirmation of many Native traditions. The very fragmentation of the Native experience in North America lends itself to a focus on context and on the artist's intentions. Marie Watt's sculpture is another metaphorical case in point. The column of blankets (Fig. 64) might be prepared for sale, or for a giveaway, except that they can't be separated from each other (they're attached by wires) even when the pile crumples and falls. Working collaboratively, with objects that bear their own histories of warmth and rejection, Watt has found a contemporary language in which to bring her Seneca culture home to wherever it is that we live. (For her it's across the country in the Northwest.)

One of the most effective weapons against stereotypes is recontextualization, where interpretation is wrenched out of the hands of those who know only Western art history and relocated in a knowledgeable home place. For instance, Cochiti Pueblo potter Diego Romero paints his traditionally shaped vessels with the cartoonlike but never jarring adventures of masked Pueblo alter egos cruising the contemporary world (Fig. 65). Diné writer Shanna Ketchum demonstrates how Romero's Chongo brothers can be equated with, or parallel, the Hero Twins of Pueblo and Navajo belief systems. Discussing the Prismacolor works of Star Wallowing Bull (Fig. 66), Ketchum appropriates Rosalind Krauss's theories on cubism to show how the artist recontextualizes Native history through formal means—illusionist and decorative forms vying for a place in a crowded pantheon, with different levels of Native and popular culture translated into transcultural space.[13]

Many Native artists have taken the stereotypes and run with them—to the point where parodies of the "noble savage," the "Indian maiden," and the "nature-identified," "earth-wise" elder are paradoxically in danger of becoming new stereotypes themselves. Obsession with the cruelties and stupidities of the dominant culture—even as it remains meaningful as a warning—is related to what we in the feminist movement used to call "being ruled by the opposition," or forced into a position that's reactive rather than proactive, cliché rather than insight. At some point it may become more challenging to construct intricate criticisms of internal as well as external problems, fueled less by individualism than by collective energy.

For years now, those of us concerned with contemporary Native art have gone around and around on the relationships between identity and culture, traditional and modernist, mainstream and marginalization. These are choices—but not the *only* choices—facing contemporary Native artists, and they are not incompatible; there is no

Fig. 63     *Table,* 2005
            Keri Ataumbi
            Cast Lucite, cast iron, and steel, 30 × 4 × 8 ft.

138

Fig. 64
*Three Sisters, Six Pelts, Cousin Rose,*
*Sky Woman and Relations,* 2004
Marie Watt
Floor-to-ceiling folded and stacked blankets
with reclaimed red cedar base

Fig. 65     *Coyote and the Disciples of Vine Deloria,* 1993
Diego Romero
Clay, paint; diam. 11⅛ in., h. 4 in.

either/or. Pretty much across the board, the best contemporary Native artists play in that liminal zone in between,
dodging the obvious contradictions and conflations. As
McNeil puts it, "My place in our American culture is a bit
off-center because I, like many other Native Americans,
really grew up outside the mainstream while simultaneously being immersed in it, which is a kind of paradox
that confuses hell out of everyone, me included . . . I see
my work as a bridge between cultures that is satirical
about both."[14]

The complex mix of personal, political, and cultural is
different for every artist. For instance, Gregory Lomayesva
(son of a Hopi father and a well-known Hispana *santera*)
was recently quoted in a magazine article: "What contemporary art really offers the maker is an individual voice that
allows you to move beyond the tribe," he says. "As a Native
artist, I'm proud of my heritage . . . But at some point,
you really do want to leave behind the need to be a 'Native
artist' and just be a person, with your own name and your
own voice." In the same article, April Tsosie (Diné) said
that she moved in a more modernist direction because she

was tired of spending so much time educating people about
her cultural background instead of "getting the critiques
I needed about the work itself."[15] Mohawk photographer
Shelley Niro suggested in 2002 that contemporary Indian
artists exist in "a vacuum that has to be filled . . . Right now,
it's just like everything is getting sucked up into that space
and I think it would be great if we were just considered
artists."[16]

I suspect that most of us who are involved in contemporary Native art can hear these statements loud and clear.
At the same time, in the phrase moving "beyond the tribe,"
we can also hear the voice of artworld individualism (or the
story of the late Fritz Scholder, who quite justifiably called
himself a non-Indian Indian but was not averse to reaping
the rewards of Native affiliation). We can also hear the call
of the wannabe and the Native reactionary who wants to
reverse history and go back to the tribe—not as it is today,
but as it once was, in a very different context. Both these
positions deny the vibrant continuum of Native culture
as it crosses and creates new thresholds, carrying with it
an identity that is both old and new. Over the centuries,

140

Fig. 66  *Mind to Mind Combat*, 2001
Star Wallowing Bull
Prismacolor pencil on paper, 22¼ × 30 in.

*Raven Contemplating the Holy Ghost,* 1996
Jeneese Hilton
Mixed media on canvas, 66 × 45 in.

ARTWORK AND DESIGN BY : STEVEN DEO
LAYOUT BY: DANYAEL LAUGHING BEAR

A PUBLIC SERVICE ANNOUNCMENT
TO RAISE AWARENESS OF
NUTRITION, LIFESTYLE AND DIABETES

*frybreadlazyboy*, 2007
Steven Deo
Lithograph, 14 × 17 in.

tribal traditions themselves have been flexible and open to change without damaging the core, and this elasticity has provided rich soil for contemporary art.

The value of "identity politics" continues to be argued in academia. It gets a bad rap because the idea is often used reductively, from the outside, as the only factor that makes Native art worth looking at. Yet the issue of identity is raised so consistently by Native artists that it's downright rude to ignore it. Creek/Seminole/Diné photographer Hulleah Tsinhnahjinnie says, "The real battle is identity."[17] And Steve Deo (Creek/Euchee) says, "Identity has been a constant point of reference for me . . . We have been relocated, dislocated, grouped and regrouped, numbered and scattered. The one commonality we have left is an extended family called 'Indian.'"[18] Deo's works expressing antiwar and anticorporate-capitalism positions tackle social issues we all face, but from a decidedly Native viewpoint. When identity is a major part of an artist's work, it should be treated as directly as it was intended before it's plunged into the theoretical melting pot. Analysis is productive if it doesn't depart from the artmakers and from the art itself.

The problem of too much attention being paid to Native identity and too little to art can and probably should be blamed on non-Indian critics/curators/cultural trespassers/colonialists who until a couple of decades ago controlled the public image of Native art (even though I personally wouldn't want to do without Jackson Rushing's or Allan Ryan's or Janet Berlo and Ruth Phillips's books).[19] But artists are also complicitous. Rampant romanticism of the past comes from several directions—from freeze-dried anthropological projects and starry-eyed art critics, but also from nostalgic Native artists. Somewhere along the line we all need to take historical responsibility for the contemporary context in which this art is made, presented, interpreted, and intended (which is easier said than done). If art is anything that an artist makes and decides to call art— a credo of the avant garde since Marcel Duchamp—then Native modernism is anything a Native artist wants to make of it. In the process maybe those other three legs will become visible, or the current three will disappear altogether.

*This is not a commercial,
this is my homeland,* 1998
Hulleah Tsinhnahjinnie
Digital photograph, dimensions
variable

## Notes

1. Loretta Todd, "What More Do They Want?" in *Indigena: Contemporary Native Perspectives,* ed. Gerald McMaster and Lee-Ann Martin (Hull, Quebec, and Vancouver, BC: Canadian Museum of Civilization and Douglas and McIntyre, 1992), 72.

2. Alfred Young Man, "The Metaphysics of North American Indian Art," in *Indigena,* 94.

3. Jean Fisher, "The Health of the People Is the Highest Law," in *Vampire in the Text* (London: InIVA, 2003), 222.

4. Olu Oguibe, "In the Heart of Darkness" (1999), quoted by Ery Camera in *A Fiction of Authenticity: Contemporary Africa Abroad,* ed. Shannon Fitzgerald and Tumelo Mosaka (St. Louis: Contemporary Art Museum, 2003), 81.

5. Bob Haozous, quoted in Lucy R. Lippard, "'Talking to Ourselves': Indian Art for Indian People," in *Bob Haozous, Indigenous Dialogue* (Santa Fe: Institute of American Indian Arts Museum, 2005), 16.

6. Anonymous Indian artist, quoted in Bruce Bernstein, "It's Art: 'Keep talking while we keep working, but hold it down so I can hear myself think,'" in *Changing Hands: Art Without Reservation 2,* ed. David R. McFadden and Ellen N. Taubman (New York: Museum of Arts and Design, 2005), 176.

7. Nancy Marie Mithlo, "Conspiracy Theory," in *Reservation X,* ed. Gerald McMaster (Seattle, WA, and Hull, Quebec: University of Washington Press and the Canadian Museum of Civilization, 1998), 135.

8. Oscar Howe, letter to Jean Snodgrass King, quoted in *Oscar Howe: A Retrospective Exhibition,* ed. Frederick J. Dockstader (Tulsa, OK: Thomas Gilcrease Museum Association, 1982), 19.

9. Mike MacDonald, quoted by Charlotte Townsend-Gault, "Let X= Audience," in *Reservation X,* 43.

10. Paul Chaat Smith, "The Meaning of Life," in *Indigena,* 40.

11. Gerald McMaster, "Living on Reservation X," in *Reservation X,* 28.

12. Keri Ataumbi, quoted in Dottie Indyke, "Keri Ataumbi," *Southwest Art,* July 2004, 53.

13. Shanna Ketchum, "Transcultural Space in Context: An Analysis of Works by Diego Romero," *Estrago* (Nicaragua, ed. Raul Quintanilla), forthcoming; and "Signs at Play in the Work of Star Wallowing Bull," in *Between Two Cultures: The Art of Star Wallowing Bull* (Fargo, ND: Plains Art Museum, 2005), 10.

14. Larry McNeil, artist's statement in *Migrations: New Directions in Native American Art,* ed. Marjorie Devon (Albuquerque: University of New Mexico Press, 2006), 87.

15. Gregory Lomayesva and April Tsosie, quoted in Gregory Pleshaw, "Artistic Identity in Native America: What's in a Label?" *Santa Fe Trend,* Spring 2005, 61–67.

16. Shelley Niro, artist's statement in *Staging the Indian: The Politics of Representation,* ed. Jill Sweet and Ian Berry (Saratoga Springs, NY: Tang Teaching Museum and Art Gallery at Skidmore College, 2002), 85.

17. Hulleah Tsinhnahjinnie, in *Image and Self in Contemporary Native American Photoart* (Hanover, NH: Dartmouth College Hood Museum of Art, 1995), 14.

18. Steve Deo, unpublished statement, n.d.

19. W. Jackson Rushing III, ed., *Native American Art in the Twentieth Century* (New York: Routledge, 1999) and his many other writings; Allan J. Ryan, *The Trickster Shift: Humour and Irony in Contemporary Native Art* (Seattle: University of Washington Press, 1999); and Janet C. Berlo and Ruth B. Phillips, *Native North American Art* (Oxford and New York: Oxford University Press, 1998).

"I Don't Feel We Did Wrong in Taking This Great
Country From Them. There Were Great Numbers
of People Who Needed New Land and
the Indians Were Selfishly Trying to
Keep It For Themselves."
                                    — John Wayne

*If we are not moved, if we stand still, the status quo is our reward. Without at least some conviction that change can be positive, the only place to go is around in circles.*

—Lucy R. Lippard[1]

For decades, artists and curators have viewed publications as a key element in their strategies to improve access to the art world and influence an individual's career. Are we-those of us who make, curate, or critique art by American Indians—projecting our proactive efforts in the right direction to gain this elusive access or turning round and round, covering the same ground over and over? It is time to take a look at what has been accomplished so we can evaluate progress and assess our strategies for positive change.

In this paper I will examine some of the landmark publications since 1990 in order to review issues of access and as a step toward broadening our goals for American Indian art. Our persistent focus on publications—especially exhibition catalogs—began as a response to the exclusion of native art not only from the art world, but from art history. Much effort has been put into this strategy, but it's an old strategy. The question now is, is it an effective strategy? Are there other, more influential actions to consider? I hope in this paper to move the dialogue about work by American Indian artists into an inclusive realm; that is, that it will be considered in the context of world art.

I begin with 1990 for two reasons. One, this was the year that Lucy R. Lippard's seminal book *Mixed Blessings* was published. *Mixed Blessings* offered a place for many artists who were making significant works but were not necessarily getting critical attention from the "mainstream" art world. Although the book had a wider focus than just American Indian artists, its presence as a major book—rather than a thin catalog—created a space that had not existed before. The text functioned as a form of validation

# Looking Back to Look Forward
*by Polly Nordstrand*

*Wayne's World,* 1992
Jesse Cooday
Mixed media on paper, 39 × 32 in.

at a time when this was vital to artists working at the margins of the center. Additionally, 1990 was about the time that some curators began to work with concentrated effort to include Indian artists in the United States' quincentennial commemoration of Columbus's arrival in the Americas. Indian artists also organized their own response to the commemoration. Not that the quincentennial was an important *art* moment, but it was a time of heightened awareness that opened the door to questioning standard methods of inclusion and representation.

*Mixed Blessings* was the exception to the rule. The major form of written documentation of American Indian art is exhibition catalogs. Frequently these are linked to group shows of American Indian artists, many of which have been organized to give a presence and a voice to Indian artists. This message has been repeatedly stated in the opening remarks of catalogs. In 1991 Martin Sullivan wrote in his foreword to the *Shared Visions: Native American Painters and Sculptors in the Twentieth Century* catalog that "there is also an element of sadness to the project in that so many important artists of Native American heritage have yet to be acknowledged by historians and critics of American fine art. By bringing together a visually stunning and emotionally powerful assemblage of works by these artists, we hope that the Native American Fine Art Movement will gain wider understanding and appreciation."[2] More than a decade later the sentiment continues to be expressed by museum directors such as John Vanausdall, who in describing the Eiteljorg Fellowship for Native American Fine Art wrote that its purpose was "to encourage and support Native American contemporary fine art and bring it the visibility it deserves."[3] Certainly the underlying purpose of *all* exhibitions is to make art available for the public to enjoy and understand, but why is this still such an overt purpose of exhibition programs of art by American Indians? Is there an equivalent statement for "mainstream" art?

Or, in repeatedly justifying American Indian exhibitions in this way are museums perpetuating a substandard position for art by American Indian artists? This message is so pervasive that it recently found its way into the final remarks of David Penney's *North American Indian Art*—a textbook geared to college art history survey courses—where future artists and scholars will read it for years to come.[4] However, curator Nancy Mithlo suggested that this approach is losing ground when she commented, "Reliance upon an inclusion/exclusion orientation results in . . . tiring and ultimately uninteresting results."[5]

*Shared Visions: Native American Painters and Sculptors in the Twentieth Century* presented the "extraordinary, but widely neglected, Native American Fine Art Movement" as it existed as of 1991.[6] In trying to define the Native American Fine Art Movement (NAFAM), Margaret Archuleta and Rennard Strickland, the curators of the exhibition, included a range of artists working throughout the century and in a variety of media, subject matter, and styles. Their primary essay in the catalog set the stage for the art presented within the context of the history of Indian policy. They then declared: "Twentieth century Indian art is about survival—the survival of the spirit."[7] They went on to say that "the Native American Fine Art Movement was born in crisis—created by an officially ordained program of cultural genocide; the homelessness of urban relocation; the bankruptcy of tribal termination; and the hopes and the frustration of Indian veterans returning from foreign wars. Over the last five or six generations, Indian painting has been in the eye of a rapidly moving whirlwind that is the Indian's struggle for survival."[8] The artists were presented as eking out a response to their terrible situation rather than using their art to participate in their contemporary world. They were presented as victims—a patronizing position. The idea that survival is the definitive purpose of their work reinforces the idea that the artists were not

*Prototype for New Understanding #11,* 2002
Brian Jungen
Nike Air Jordans, human hair, 26½ × 23 × 10 in.

*blood on the snow,* 2002
Rebecca Belmore
Installation, 3 ft. 6 in. × 20 ft. × 20 ft.
Courtesy of the Morris and Helen Belkin
Art Gallery; Photographer: Howard Ursuliak

successful. But the idea of a "movement" never entirely took hold. Although Penney made a reference to the "American Indian Fine Arts Movement" in his textbook, the term is not widely used in discussions of art history.[9] Can we expect that the larger society, which focuses so heavily on advancement, will relate to art about survival? Is the position that American Indian art is about survival a reason that the concept of this movement never fully engaged many art historians?

Within the context of survival, Archuleta and Strickland defined the artist as "recorder, conveyor, and preserver of traditional values in the midst of social change." They discussed the diverse subjects of the work as the spectrum of Indian culture from "daily tasks" to "myths and legends."[10] They concluded that "Indian paintings are true sources for insight into Indian culture," yet later lamented, "Why is Indian fine art almost never seen and, when exhibited, often viewed only as an adjunct to Indian arts and crafts shows or as ethnographic specimens in museums of natural history?"[11] It makes sense that we can't have it both ways. Is there another model that allows us to recognize the multiple approaches of artists from illustrative to nonobjective in order to better clarify work by Indian artists? Would it help the viewer—not to mention the critics—to present the work in a context that makes it relevant to the "mainstream" art world rather than continue to wonder why the work is not exhibited and appreciated? This is not to say that we ignore the significance of the works to Indian audiences, who are often sensitive to the artists' intentions because of common experiences, but that we also need to develop methods that sort out the significance of the works for multiple audiences.

Artists need to be seen for what they are doing more than for the lives that they are living. Lippard emphasized the artist's role in shaping society when she wrote: "Visual artists are conscious, and unconscious, agents of mass

dreams, allowing forbidden or forgotten images to surface, reinforcing aspects of identity that provide pride and self-esteem, countering the malignant imprint of socially imposed inferiority."[12] We need to see artists as more than recorders; we need to see their work as an impetus to move society forward.

Archuleta and Strickland also believe that artists have the power to provide positive change in society: "These artists can help in understanding the universal challenge of responding to cultural and technological change."[13] This observation is significant in discussing the work of American Indian artists and perhaps is one key reason why it is crucial to promote and exhibit the work of these artists. Artist and historian Jolene Rickard reiterated this point in the proceedings of "Vision, Space, Desire," a symposium held in 2005: "I argue that indigenous people globally do have something very important to contribute on the cusp of the twenty-first century. We have densely packed cultural survival kits that transfer knowledge from one generation to the next, despite unremitting attempts at genocide, culturalcide, and other forms of political and philosophical erasure."[14] If all that is accomplished by exhibitions and publications is gaining access within the art world, I don't believe that we will know the real impact of indigenous artists nor fully understand what lies beyond basic survival.

In *Shared Visions,* Jackson Rushing pointed to the power of artists to shift societal thinking when he stated: "With the visual arts now conceived as a form of discourse shaped by cultural and historical factors, there has been a 'movement from analysis of artistic products toward consideration of the production of meaning.'"[15] He went on to examine Fritz Scholder and T. C. Cannon as postmodernists who deconstruct the representation of Indians in portraiture. Rushing's essay discussed the artists' work in the context of art theory and established their importance not

Fig. 67    *Metissage,* 1995
Teresa Marshall
Cedar, tobacco, four stone needles; h. 138 in., diam. 51½ in.

only in Indian art, but also in the larger art world and society. He showed these artists as agents of change, not simply victims of circumstance. But decades after the acclaim that Scholder and Cannon have garnered, what other artists have achieved the platform to speak beyond the close circle of friends of Indian art?

It is time to look at the messages that those of us involved with native arts project and ask whether we have told ourselves—and others—the same disparaging words so many times that we now accept them as true. Do we perpetuate the victim position for which we reproach the "mainstream"? The statements about being ignored, being treated as simple, and about "we are still here" seem endless—and powerless. I believe that there has always been resistance to this mindset. Since the beginnings of the Native American Fine Art Movement, artists and curators have made decisions that worked against victimization, and they continue to do so. Counter—or perhaps complementary—to the assessment that Indian art is about survival, Colleen Cutschall's discussion of Teresa Marshall's work in the Eiteljorg's first exhibition of fellowship recipients, *After the Storm,* identified the potent visual text that Marshall creates in her art as possessing the enduring ability to communicate across cultures: "The visual and cultural language that Marshall utilizes with humor, strategic precision, and dexterity recalls the historically high incidence of multilingualism among aboriginal nations."[16] Marshall's *Metissage* (Fig. 67)—an oversize thread spool and four foot-long stone needles—commands attention as a sculptural installation while suggesting the enormous role that sewing plays in women's livelihood. Some might call this duality Marshall's ability to "live in two worlds," while others might theorize that she participates in a postmodern disruption of the "grand narrative." It is time to start recognizing ourselves as negotiators—with multilingual dexterity—for our cultural relevance and to abandon

alienating sentiments that Indians are only understood by other Indians, such as those expressed by Gail Tremblay in *Native Modernism: The Art of George Morrison and Allan Houser*: "The need to see indigenous culture survive that fueled the works of so many early painters of the Oklahoma and Santa Fe Schools gives those works an importance that few non-Native art critics will ever understand."[17] It is time to put our skills and insight to use in writing the critical and historical analysis that we find lacking.

## The Role of Criticism

Undeniably there has been minimal critical review of Native American art by the art world. Recognition of this void was one of the initial comments made in a 1992 volume of *Art Journal,* coedited by Jackson Rushing and Kay WalkingStick, on recent Native American art during the flourishing of possibilities that appeared around the quincentennial. WalkingStick stated: "Not to receive serious critical review is a kind of disempowerment."[18] In 1999, Margaret Dubin observed that "reviews tend to read more like reports than critiques"[19] and offered the explanation that this is due to there being few critics who specialize in American Indian contemporary art. She went on to say, "In the absence of an accepted strategy for evaluation, the overwhelming majority of writing is concerned not with judgment, but with the maintenance and reconciliation of difference."[20] But what of the overall state of art criticism today? Jerry Saltz, critic for the *Village Voice,* affirmed that the majority of art critics are unwilling to participate in the judging of art: "They praise everything they see, or only describe." The result of this reluctance, Saltz said, "sells everyone short and is creating a real disconnect."[21] Despite the pervasiveness of "no-risk non-criticism," Saltz did not believe that "post-criticism" is possible—as humans we all make judgments. Some critics point to the "anything goes" attitude of an increasingly "pluralistic" art world as the root cause of art criticism's downward spiral of influence.[22] The first time that I heard that art criticism was over, it reminded me of the museum curator's cry against opening the field to a nonacademic approach that valued indigenous knowledge—now that participation in the global art world is widening, the art critics are going to deny access by declaring their discipline obsolete.

Whatever caused the so-called crisis in art criticism for the "mainstream" may have been similar or different for Indian art, so maybe it is more important to identify what it is that we expect from art criticism or reporting. Are we seeking attention or criticism? Are we looking for a mere presence in the press or affirmation that the work being done by Indian artists is good / important? As a critic, Saltz says he looks for "originality, surprise, obsession, energy, experimentation, something visionary."[23] Are these the criteria that we set for Indian artists? You could probably divide a room by those who want tradition versus those who want originality.

Facing these issues, how do we start to participate in the process of criticism so that we bring attention to the powerful contributions to world art being made by Indian artists? Another participant in the "Vision, Space, Desire" symposium, Nancy Mithlo, suggested that criticism is an "aesthetic discourse." Just as artists Allan Houser and T. C. Cannon integrated ideas and aesthetic approaches into their work in order to construct new representations of Indians, we need to engage with the world art forum to create a place for the aesthetic being created by Indian artists. In Mithlo's words, "the purpose of contemporary Native arts criticism in a more proactive frame of reference is less about what others think (getting in and being witnessed by others as in a ceremony) and more about what we think of ourselves in relationship with others." She recommends "repositioning the conversation" and

envisions a "culturally specific platform that is simultaneously engaged with larger art currents [that] can emerge if space is made available outside of the standardized inclusion / legitimization agenda."[24]

## Engaging in Art History

This repositioning needs to address our efforts in creating an art history about American Indian artists. The lack of attention paid by art historians to Indian artists has resulted in the rise in importance of the exhibition catalog as a means of documentation. Largely geared toward popular taste and popularizing native art, these catalogs are not a substitute for the historical research and theoretical work that needs to be done. This work needs to come from scholars who are intimate with native history and world views; scholars who can offer informed perspectives about the context of the work—whether they are Indian scholars or not. Dubin remarked, "The challenge in writing about Native American art is to recognize areas of difference, as well as areas of merging social and cultural practices, as they coexist within and influence the nature of our shared modernity."[25] She called for historians and critics of Western art to apply the same standards of aesthetic judgment to art by American Indians. We must also exert effort to be as *inclusive* as we want to be *included*. Lippard said of her own approach to inclusivity, "we can choose instead [of exclusion] to learn to read the unfamiliar symbols and images buried in the experiences of others, to share the development of a fresh outlook—or an *inlook,* a vision."[26]

In their final chapter of *Native North American Art,* Janet Berlo and Ruth Phillips address the twentieth century. In defining art from this time period they note that they "use the term 'modern' somewhat differently than do historians of Western art. For Native art, we propose, the modern is defined not by a particular set of stylistic

153

*Jingle, Jingle,* 1997
Judith Lowry
Acrylic on canvas, 69¾ × 46½ in.

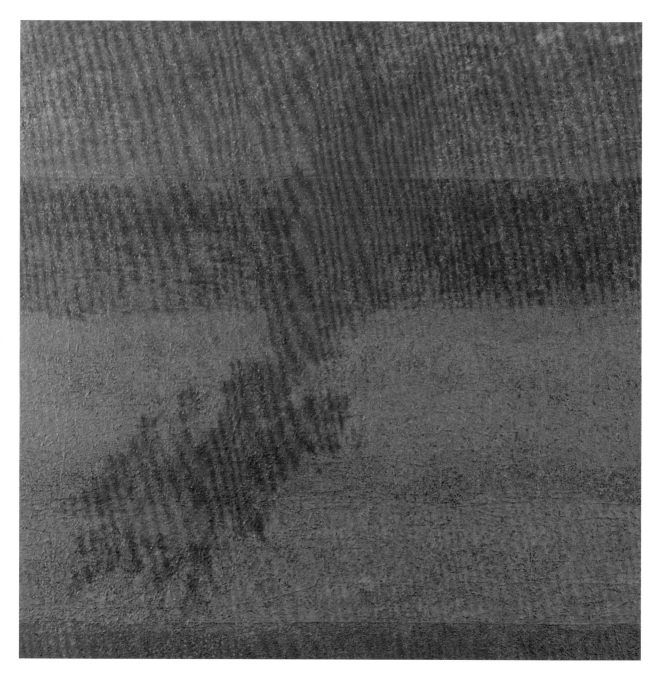

*Untitled (Lake Superior),* 1986
George Morrison
Oil on canvas, 48 × 48 in.

or conceptual categories, but by the adoption of Western representational styles, genres, and media in order to produce works that function as autonomous entities and that are intended to be experienced independently from community or ceremonial contexts."[27] What is the purpose of changing the meaning of the category when applying it to Indian artists? It is stating that they do not legitimately belong in the category. Rather than work to define what has taken place in the history of American Indian art, the authors fabricate a pseudo-explanation: "Native engagement with twentieth-century art produced a number of 'modernisms' rather than a single monolithic style."[28] Mithlo sees this as counterproductive: "A fundamental break in understanding occurs when only select conceptual categories are at play—postmodernism, conceptual, and traditional. Recognition of cultural specificity is essential at this point."[29]

When the National Museum of the American Indian presented *Native Modernism: The Art of George Morrison and Allan Houser* in 2004 as an inaugural exhibit of the new museum, the curators sought to celebrate these two accomplished artists and to find the native influences in their two very different pursuits of modernism. Curator Truman Lowe asserted that these artists "hold important places in and for the history of recent Native American art."[30] Later in his introduction to the catalog Lowe wrote, "My hope is that this book and exhibition will inspire further examination and reevaluation of the art of George Morrison and Allan Houser, and of the profound change their work has wrought on the history of American and Native American art."[31] Why is it necessary to "hope" that someone else will do this full examination of the achievements of these artists and their place in the context of world art history? If we leave the work of inclusion to others, we will continue to drain our energy with the continued yearning rather than replenishing ourselves with the creative action of identifying the movements and genres that embrace and are born of the achievements of native artists.

The question of inclusion is complicated by the splintering of "mainstream" art. "We see contemporary Indian art in the sixties entering the context of White culture at a moment when the pillars of modernism are crumbling and the dominant culture is in a state of crisis," German scholar Gerhard Hoffmann wrote.[32] He summarized possible results of the "delegitimized" Western cultures from the postmodern theorist position: "The result . . . is a concept of a pluralistic society and culture. One can argue that this pluralism leads to [1] the radical hedonistic eclecticism of 'anything goes' and ultimately to an attitude of radical indifference . . . [2] socially responsible consensus, equality and unity. Or [3] one can finally celebrate this pluralistic diversity as something 'vital' and dynamic, seeing in it a sign of the breaking down of intellectual and cultural barriers and polarities."[33] Do we lament this "anything goes" art-world opportunity, as those art critics who see it as threatening their very basis for existence do? Was Indian art just on the cusp of recognition when it was enveloped within the ever-growing pool of pluralism? When Indian artists and scholars grumble that Indian art is not understood or appreciated, do we back away from the indifference out of frustration? Is this the fate of the multicultural art world predicted in *Mixed Blessings*? Or do we now use the foundation that we've set to move forward with the confident knowledge that native artists are doing work that is highly relevant to the burgeoning pluralism?

Is it time to move away from "Indian" and focus on art? Critic Raphael Rubinstein wrote that "classification, some might argue, is the only viable response to a pluralistic era, when there is no prevalent style or shared set of esthetic criteria."[34] Gerhard Hoffmann in part agreed when he

  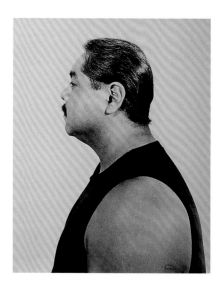

*Half Indian / Half Mexican,* 1991
James Luna
Gelatin silver prints, in three parts, 30 × 24 in. each

commented, "In view of the diversity of individual approaches, 'Indian' art can be nothing more than a vague—albeit necessary—construct that serves to emphasize certain shared characteristics."[35] Artist Kay WalkingStick contended that "separation seems to reduce the possibilities of serious critical discourse, and thus implies that there are different standards for different people . . . Separate is still not equal; it marginalizes the art."[36] In her research findings, *A Separate Vision: Case Studies of Four Contemporary Indian Artists,* Linda Eaton observed that "this practice of lumping all Indian artists, past and present, together experientially allows Indian art to be often misunderstood and lumped together as well, and creates the side-category 'Indian Art' in such a way that it covertly denies the existence of each artist's unique vision."[37] Can we break apart this lump to better understand the impact of these works within the larger context of world art and interpret Indian art as influential instead of a reaction to Western culture—or worse yet an unrelated sidebar? Can we identify true movements and aesthetics in the history of art by American Indians?

Unfortunately, the narrow deciding factors of Indianness—blood quantum and land boundaries—create a narrow-minded perception of what is Indian. Once while researching files in the National Archives from the early agency days I came across a set of correspondence papers in which an individual was petitioning to become a member of his tribe. He had worked out with the "chiefs" that one condition of his enrollment would be that he would give them each a certain number of cattle from his herd. Agreeing to this, he sought confirmation from the Indian Agent. In conclusion the Indian Agent decided that this individual was too successful (a land owner and farmer) to be an "Indian." This definition of Indian was new to me— that in the early 1900s "Indian" meant ward of the state— and opened my eyes to how Indians are seen and sometimes see themselves. But this is not how I have ever seen myself. We cannot overlook the fact that Indian people have fought hard in the twentieth century to maintain their cultural and political identities as Indians. Nor can we ignore the significance of the notion of survival in Indian world views. The question is, how do we reposition the conversation so that we can break away from the circular pattern of thinking and reveal the impact of Indian artists?

# Notes

1. Lucy R. Lippard, *Mixed Blessings: New Art in a Multicultural America* (New York: Pantheon Books, 1990), 11.

2. Martin Sullivan, foreword to *Shared Visions: Native American Painters and Sculptors in the Twentieth Century,* ed. Margaret Archuleta and Rennard Strickland (Phoenix: Heard Museum, 1991), 3.

3. John Vanausdall, quoted in *After the Storm: The Eiteljorg Fellowship for Native American Fine Art, 2001,* ed. W. Jackson Rushing III (Indianapolis: Eiteljorg Museum of American Indians and Western Art, 2001), xi.

4. David W. Penney, *North American Indian Art* (London: Thames & Hudson, 2004), 212.

5. Nancy Mithlo, "'Give, Give, Giving': Cultural Translations," in *Vision, Space, Desire: Global Perspectives and Cultural Hybridity* (Washington, DC: National Museum of the American Indian, Smithsonian Institution, 2006), 93.

6. Sullivan, foreword to *Shared Visions,* 3.

7. Margaret Archuleta and Rennard Strickland, "The Way People Were Meant to Live," in *Shared Visions,* 7.

8. Ibid, 7.

9. Penney, *North American Indian Art,* 201.

10. Archuleta and Strickland, "The Way People Were Meant to Live," 7.

11. Ibid, 9.

12. Lippard, *Mixed Blessings,* 40.

13. Archuleta and Strickland, "The Way People Were Meant to Live," 10.

14. Jolene Rickard, "The Local and the Global," in *Vision, Space, Desire,* 66.

15. W. Jackson Rushing III, "Authenticity and Subjectivity in Post-War Painting: Concerning Herrera, Scholder, and Cannon," in *Shared Visions,* 15. The second half of Rushing's comment quotes Kate Linker, "Representation and Sexuality," in *Art after Modernism: Rethinking Representation,* ed. Brian Wallis, 391–2 (New York and Boston: New Museum of Contemporary Art and D. R. Godine, 1984).

16. Colleen Cutschall, "Teresa Marshall: 'Wear the Media' Is the Message," in *After the Storm,* 50.

17. Gail Tremblay, "Different Paths: Tracks Worth Following," in *Native Modernism: The Art of George Morrison and Allan Houser,* ed. Truman T. Lowe (Washington, DC, and Seattle: National Museum of the American Indian, Smithsonian Institution, in association with University of Washington Press, 2004), 88.

18. Kay WalkingStick, "Native American Art in the Postmodern Era," *Art Journal* 51, no. 3 (Fall 1992): 15.

19. Margaret Dubin, "Sanctioned Scribes: How Critics and Historians Write the Native American Art World," in *Native American Art in the Twentieth Century,* ed. W. Jackson Rushing III (New York: Routledge, 1999), 157.

20. Ibid, 159.

21. Jerry Saltz, "Seeing Out Loud: Having an Eye in Criticism Is as Important as Having an Ear in Music," *Village Voice,* December 16, 2005.

22. Raphael Rubinstein, "A Quiet Crisis," *Art in America,* March 2003, 39–45.

23. Saltz, "Seeing Out Loud."

24. Mithlo, "'Give, Give, Giving': Cultural Translations," 88–89.

25. Dubin, "Sanctioned Scribes," 161.

26. Lippard, *Mixed Blessings,* 245.

27. Janet C. Berlo and Ruth B. Phillips, *Native North American Art* (Oxford and New York: Oxford University Press, 1998), 210.

28. Ibid, 223.

29. Mithlo, "'Give, Give, Giving': Cultural Translations," 92.

30. Truman T. Lowe, "The Emergence of Native Modernism," in *Native Modernism,* 10.

31. Ibid, 37.

32. Gerhard Hoffmann, "Postmodern Culture and Indian Art," in *In the Shadow of the Sun: Perspectives on Contemporary Native Art* (Hull, Quebec: Canadian Museum of Civilization, 1993), 259.

33. Ibid, 261.

34. Rubinstein, "A Quiet Crisis," 39.

35. Hoffmann, "Postmodern Culture and Indian Art," 257.

36. WalkingStick, "Native American Art in the Postmodern Era," 15.

37. Linda Eaton, *A Separate Vision: Case Studies of Four Contemporary Indian Artists,* Museum of Northern Arizona Bulletin 58 (Flagstaff: Museum of Northern Arizona Press, 1990), 1.

# Contributors

Nancy J. Blomberg is Senior Curator and Head of the Native Arts Department at the Denver Art Museum where she oversees the acquisition, preservation, research and interpretation of the American Indian, African, and Oceanic collections. Prior to Denver she was curator at the Los Angeles County Museum of Natural History. Her research specialties include North American Indian art and cultures —specifically Navajo textiles. Her major books include: *Navajo Textiles: The William Randolph Hearst Collection* (1988) and *Breaking the Mold: The Virginia Vogel Mattern Collection of Contemporary Native American Art* (2006) coauthor.

HOCK E AYE VI Edgar Heap of Birds received his M.F.A. from Tyler School of Art, Temple University, Philadelphia; his B.F.A. from the University of Kansas, Lawrence; and has undertaken graduate studies at the Royal College of Art, London.

The artworks of Heap of Birds include multidisciplinary forms of public art messages, large-scale drawings, *Neuf* series acrylic paintings, prints, and monumental porcelain enamel on steel outdoor sculpture. He has exhibited his works at (among others) the Museum of Modern Art, Whitney Museum of American Art, National Museum of the American Indian, the National Gallery of Canada, the Museum of Contemporary Art, Sydney, and the Venice Biennale, 2007. Professor Heap of Birds teaches Native American Studies and Fine Arts at the University of Oklahoma.

Lucy Lippard is an internationally acclaimed writer and activist and the author of more than twenty books on art and cultural criticism. She has been the recipient of numerous awards for her work including the Guggenheim Foundation, the National Endowment for the Arts, and the College Art Association. Her two most recent books are titled *Lure of the Local: Senses of Place in a Multicentered Society* (1997) and *Off the Beaten Track: Tourism, Art, and Place* (1999). Ms. Lippard lives in Galisteo, New Mexico.

Nancy Marie Mithlo, Ph.D., is Assistant Professor of Art History at the University of Wisconsin, Madison. Mithlo's research addresses the emerging field of indigenous museum curatorial methods as a component of an indigenous knowledge systems approach. The manner in which visual records (photo, film, computer-generated images) as well as arts and material culture are managed, appropriated, and strategically put to use in politically charged areas serves as the focal point for her research. As the Director of the Indigenous Arts Action Alliance, she brought Native art exhibits to the Venice Biennale in 1999, 2001, 2003, and 2007.

Polly Nordstrand is Associate Curator of American Indian art in the Native Arts Department at the Denver Art Museum. She recently curated the exhibits *Maria: American Icon* and *Fonseca's Coyote: Living with the Trickster*. She is the coauthor of *Breaking the Mold: The Virginia Vogel Mattern Collection of Contemporary Native American Art,* an accompanying catalogue for the exhibit of the same title. Previously she was curator of collections and exhibits at Ah Tah Thi Ki Museum, of the Seminole Tribe of Florida, and a researcher for the National Museum of the American Indian. She regularly lectures about American Indian art history and museum studies at the University of Colorado and the University of Denver.

W. Jackson Rushing III is Adkins Presidential Professor of Art History at the University of Oklahoma, where he holds the Carver Chair in Native American Art. His books include *Native American Art and the New York Avant-Garde: A History of Cultural Primitivism* (The University of Texas Press, 1995) and *Allan Houser: An American Master* (Harry N. Abrams, 2004). He has been a Fellow of the Howard Foundation, the Guggenheim Foundation, and the National Endowment for the Humanities. His art criticism has appeared in *American Craft, American Indian Art Magazine, Art Journal, Art on Paper, Flash Art, New Art Examiner, Sculpture,* and *Third Text.*

Alfred Young Man, Ph.D. (Eagle Chief), is a Cree Professor and Department Head of Indian Fine Arts at First Nations University of Canada, Regina, Saskatchewan. He was born in Browning, Montana, on the Blackfeet Indian Reservation in 1948. Major published works include: *Kiskayetum: Allan Sapp, a Retrospective* (Mackenzie Art Gallery, 1994); *North American Indian Art: It's a Question of Integrity* (Kamloops Art Gallery, 1998), and *You Are in Indian Country: A Native Perspective on Native Arts/Politics* (Banff Press, 2007).

## Image Credits

Page 32
*New Growth,* 1995
Gordon Hookey
Acrylic on canvas
24 × 30 in.
Image courtesy of Edgar Heap of Birds

Page 33
*P.T.O. (Please Turn Over),* 2000
Beezy Bailey; A Public Eye Project
Art intervention
Image courtesy of Edgar Heap of Birds

Page 34
Big Horn Medicine Wheel,
Wyoming, 1999
Photographer: Edgar Heap of Birds
Image courtesy of Edgar Heap of Birds

Page 35
Sun Dance Lodge and Medicine Wheel
Brown Reference Group

Page 37
*Wheel, Tree 10,* 2005
Edgar Heap of Birds
Porcelain on steel
144 × 24 × 24 in.
Denver Art Museum Collection,
1997.1452.10; © Denver Art Museum

Selected Works of HOCK E
AYE VI Edgar Heap of Birds
Page 38
*Untitled,* 1974
Edgar Heap of Birds
Acrylic on canvas
6 × 6 ft.
Image courtesy of the artist

Page 39
*Construction,* 1976
Edgar Heap of Birds
Mixed media installation
8 × 12 ft.
Image courtesy of the artist

Page 41
*Kiowa Memorial,* 1976
Edgar Heap of Birds, Don Secondine
Horse hair, acrylic paint, cedar branches,
and single tree
25 ft.
Image courtesy of Edgar Heap of Birds

Page 42
*London Shape,* 1977
Edgar Heap of Birds
Acrylic paint on illustration board
12 × 16 ft.
Image courtesy of the artist

*Howling Crane,* 1977
Edgar Heap of Birds
Serigraph
24 × 36 in.
Image courtesy of the artist

Page 43
*Red Dirt Contrast,* 1978
Edgar Heap of Birds
Tempera on paper
36 × 49 in.
Image courtesy of the artist

Page 44
*Win of Birds,* 1978
Edgar Heap of Birds
Mixed media on paper
24 × 36 in.
Image courtesy of the artist

Page 45
*Boil Broken Bones,* 1979
Edgar Heap of Birds
Acrylic paint and photographs on canvas
8 × 8 ft.
Image courtesy of the artist

Page 46
*Powwow Chair,* 1979
Edgar Heap of Birds
Aluminum lawn chair, Pendleton
blanket, and Oklahoma earth
48 × 48 in.
Image courtesy of the artist

Page 47
*Fort Marion Lizards,* 1979
Edgar Heap of Birds
Acrylic on wall board
8 × 8 ft.
Image courtesy of the artist

Page 49
*Neuf Series #1,* 1981
Edgar Heap of Birds
Acrylic on canvas board
8 × 10 in.
Image courtesy of the artist

Page 50
*Don't Want Indians,* 1982
Edgar Heap of Birds
Die-cut letters on wall
8 × 5 ft.
Image courtesy of the artist

Page 51
*In Our Language,* 1982
Edgar Heap of Birds
Computer light billboard
20 × 40 ft.
Image courtesy of the artist

Page 52
*Death from the Top,* 1983
Edgar Heap of Birds
Painted die-cut letters on wall
8 × 20 ft.
Image courtesy of the artist

Page 53
*South African Homelands,* 1986
Edgar Heap of Birds
Painted stencil text mural on wall
8 × 20 ft.
Image courtesy of the artist

Page 54
*Telling Many Magpies, Telling Black Wolf,
Telling Hachivi,* 1989
Edgar Heap of Birds
Serigraph
62 × 42 in.
Image courtesy of the artist

Page 56
*Apartheid Oklahoma,* 1989
Edgar Heap of Birds
Billboard, ink on paper
5 × 9 ft.
Image courtesy of the artist

Page 57
*Mission Gifts,* 1990
Edgar Heap of Birds
Paper bus banner
3 × 9 ft.
Image courtesy of the artist

Page 58
*Building Minnesota,* 1990
Edgar Heap of Birds
Screen printing on metal panels
18 × 36 in. each; 400-ft. outdoor
installation
Image courtesy of the artist

Page 59
*Learn a War Cry,* 1994
Edgar Heap of Birds, Fiona Foley
Mylar text on wall
8 × 7 ft.
Image courtesy of Edgar Heap of Birds

Page 60
*American Leagues,* 1996
Edgar Heap of Birds
Commercial billboard
6 × 12 ft.
Image courtesy of the artist

Page 61
*Dunging the Ground,* 1996
Edgar Heap of Birds
Mylar text on steel panels
42 × 60 in. each
Image courtesy of the artist

Page 62
*Neuf Series,* 1997
Edgar Heap of Birds
Acrylic on canvas
89 × 105 in.
Image courtesy of the artist

Page 63
*You May Enter,* 2004
Edgar Heap of Birds
Monoprint
22 × 15 in.
Image courtesy of the artist

Page 64
Ocmulgee exhibition
Atlanta College of Art
March 10–April 24, 2005
Image courtesy of Edgar Heap of Birds

163

Page 143
*This is not a commercial, this is my homeland,* 1998
Hulleah Tsinhnahjinnie
Digital photograph
Dimensions variable
Image courtesy of the artist

Chapter 6
Page 144
*Wayne's World,* 1992
Jesse Cooday
Mixed media on paper
39 × 32 in.
Denver Art Museum Collection:
Genevieve D. Searle Fund, 2002.92;
© Denver Art Museum

Page 147
*Prototype for New Understanding #11,* 2002
Brian Jungen
Nike Air Jordans, human hair
26½ × 23 × 10 in.
Collection of Gilles and Julia Ouellette, Toronto; Courtesy Catriona Jeffries Gallery, Vancouver

Page 148
*blood on the snow,* 2002
Rebecca Belmore
Installation
3 ft. 6 in. × 20 ft. × 20 ft.
Courtesy of the Morris and Helen Belkin Art Gallery; Photographer: Howard Ursuliak

Page 150
*Metissage,* 1995
Teresa Marshall
Cedar, tobacco, four stone needles
H. 138 in., diam. 51½ in.
Courtesy of the Eiteljorg Museum of American Indians and Western Art, Indianapolis

Page 153
*Jingle, Jingle,* 1997
Judith Lowry
Acrylic on canvas
69¾ × 46½ in.
Denver Art Museum Collection:
Native Arts acquisition funds, 2007.48;
© Denver Art Museum

Page 154
*Untitled (Lake Superior),* 1986
George Morrison
Oil on canvas
48 × 48 in.
From the collection of the Minnesota Museum of American Art, Katharine Ordway Fund Purchase

Page 156
*Half Indian / Half Mexican,* 1991
James Luna
Gelatin silver prints, in three parts
30 × 24 in. each
Denver Art Museum Collection:
Native Arts acquisition funds,
2007.43 a,b,c; © Denver Art Museum

## Selected Bibliography

Alcoff, Linda Martin. "Who's Afraid of Identity Politics?" In *Reclaiming Identity: Realist Theory and the Predicament of Post-modernism,* editcd by Paula M. L. Moya and Michael R. Hames-Garcia. Berkeley: University of California Press, 2000.

Archuleta, Margaret, and Rennard Strickland. "The Way People Were Meant to Live." In Archuleta and Strickland, *Shared Visions.*

———, eds. *Shared Visions: Native American Painters and Sculptors in the Twentieth Century.* Phoenix: Heard Museum, 1991.

Berkhofer, Robert F. Jr. *The White Man's Indian: Images of the American Indian from Columbus to the Present.* New York: Vintage Books, 1979.

Berlo, Janet Catherine, ed. *Plains Indian Drawings, 1865–1935: Pages from a Visual History.* New York: Harry N. Abrams, 1996.

Berlo, Janet C., and Ruth B. Phillips. *Native North American Art.* Oxford and New York: Oxford University Press, 1998.

Bernstein, Bruce. "It's Art: 'Keep talking while we keep working, but hold it down so I can hear myself think.'" In *Changing Hands: Art Without Reservation 2,* edited by David R. McFadden and Ellen N. Taubman. New York: Museum of Arts and Design, 2005.

Bernstein, Bruce, and Gerald McMaster. *First American Art: The Charles and Valerie Diker Collection of American Indian Art.* Washington, DC: Smithsonian National Museum of the American Indian in association with the University of Washington Press, 2004.

Bieder, Robert. "Anthropology and History of the American Indian." *American Quarterly* 33, no. 3 (1981): 309–26.

Connolly, Mark R. "What's in a Name? A Historical Look at Native American–Related Nicknames and Symbols at Three U.S. Universities." *Journal of Higher Education* 71, no. 5 (2000): 515–47.

Cutschall, Colleen. "Teresa Marshall: 'Wear the Media' Is the Message." In Rushing, *After the Storm.*

Day, Holliday T. *"He says, She says."* Omaha, NE: Joslyn Art Museum, 1982.

Deloria, Philip. *Indians in Unexpected Places.* Lawrence: University Press of Kansas, 2004.

Deloria, Vine Jr. *Custer Died for Your Sins: An Indian Manifesto.* New York: Avon Books, 1969.

Dockstader, Frederick J. *Indian Art in America: The Arts and Crafts of the North American Indian.* Greenwich, CT: New York Graphic Society, 1961.

———, ed. *Oscar Howe: A Retrospective Exhibition.* Tulsa, OK: Thomas Gilcrease Museum Association, 1982.

Douglas, Mary. *Purity and Danger: An Analysis of Concepts of Pollution and Taboo.* London: Ark Paperbacks, 1966.

Dubin, Margaret. "Sanctioned Scribes: How Critics and Historians Write the Native American Art World." In Rushing, *Native American Art in the Twentieth Century.*

Durham, Jimmie. "A Central Margin." In *The Decade Show: Frameworks of Identity in the 1980s.* New York: Museum of Contemporary Hispanic Art, New Museum of Contemporary Art, and Studio Museum of Harlem, 1990.

Eaton, Linda. *A Separate Vision: Case Studies of Four Contemporary Indian Artists.* Museum of Northern Arizona Bulletin 58. Flagstaff: Museum of Northern Arizona Press, 1990.

Eldridge, Laurie. "Dorothy Dunn and the Art Education of Native Americans: Continuing the Dialogue." *Studies in Art Education* 42, no. 4 (2001): 318–32.

Fisher, Jean. "The Health of the People Is the Highest Law." In *Vampire in the Text* (London: InIVA, 2003).

Foster, Hal, ed. *The Anti-Aesthetic: Essays on Postmodern Culture.* Port Townsend, WA: Bay Press, 1983.

Garroutte, Eva Marie. "The Racial Formation of American Indians: Negotiating Legitimate Identities within Tribal and Federal Law." *American Indian Quarterly* 25, no. 2 (2001): 224–39.

General, David. "Indian Artists or Artists Who Are Indian?" *Native Perspective Magazine* (National Association of Friendship Centres, Ottawa) 3, no. 2 (1978).

Godfrey, Tony. *Conceptual Art.* London: Phaidon, 1998.

Green, Rayna. "The Indian in Popular American Culture." In *Handbook of North American Indians,* edited by William C. Sturtevant. Vol. 4, *History of Indian-White Relations.* Washington, DC: Smithsonian Institution Press, 1988.

———. "The Pocahontas Perplex." In *Unequal Sisters: A Multicultural Reader in U.S. Women's History,* edited by Ellen Carol DuBois and Vicki L. Ruiz. New York: Routledge, 1990.

Handler, Richard. "Is 'Identity' a Useful Concept?" *In Commemorations: The Politics of National Identity,* edited by John R. Gillis. Princeton, NJ: Princeton University Press, 1994.

Hanson, Jeffrey R., and Linda P. Rouse. "American Indian Stereotyping, Resource Competition, and Status-based Prejudice." *American Indian Culture and Research Journal* 15, no. 3 (1991): 1–17.

———. "Dimensions of Native American Stereotyping." *American Indian Culture and Research Journal* 11, no. 4 (1987): 33–58.

Harris, Michael. *Colored Pictures: Race and Visual Representation.* Chapel Hill: University of North Carolina Press, 2003.

Harrison, Faye. "Unraveling Race for the Twenty-First Century." In *Exotic No More: Anthropology on the Frontlines,* edited by Jeremy MacClancy. Chicago: University of Chicago Press, 2002.

Heap of Birds, Edgar. "Insurgent Messages for America." *Afterimage* 14 (October 1986); reprinted in *Claim Your Color,* Papo Colo et al. New York: Exit Art, 1989.

———. "Of Circularity and Linearity in the Work of Bear's Heart." In Berlo, *Plains Indian Drawings, 1865–1935.*

———. Artist's statement for *Building Minnesota. Caliban* 8 (1990): 81.

———. Artist's statement in *Hachivi Edgar Heap of Birds: MATRIX 131,* edited by Andrea Miller-Keller. Hartford, CT: Wadsworth Atheneum Museum of Art, 1996.

———. Artist's statement in *Word/Image: The Art of Reading,* by Barrett Watten. San Francisco: New Langston Art, 1985.

Highwater, Jamake. "Heap of Birds." *Native Arts/West,* April 1981.

———. *Song from the Earth: American Indian Painting.* Boston: New York Graphic Society, 1976.

Hoffmann, Gerhard. "Postmodern Culture and Indian Art." In *In the Shadow of the Sun: Perspectives on Contemporary Native Art.* Hull, Quebec: Canadian Museum of Civilization, 1993.

Houle, Robert. "The Struggle against Cultural Apartheid." *Muse* (Canadian Museums Association, Ottawa), fall 1988.

Houle, Robert, and Carol Podedworny. *Mandate Study 1990–93: An Investigation of Issues Surrounding the Exhibition, Collection and Interpretation of Contemporary Art by First Nations Artists.* Thunder Bay, Canada: Thunder Bay Art Gallery, 1994.

Indyke, Dottie. "Keri Ataumbi." *Southwest Art,* July 2004.

Jessup, Lynda, and Shannon Bagg, eds. *On Aboriginal Representation in the Gallery.* Hull, Quebec: Canadian Museum of Civilization, 2002.

Ketchum, Shanna. "Signs at Play in the Work of Star Wallowing Bull." In *Between Two Cultures: The Art of Star Wallowing Bull.* Fargo, ND: Plains Art Museum, 2005.

———. "Transcultural Space in Context: An Analysis of Works by Diego Romero." *Estrago* (Nicaragua, edited by Raul Quintanilla), forthcoming.

King, C. Richard. "Bad Anthropologies: Scholars, Sports Fans, and Native American Mascots," *InterCulture* (Florida State University Dept. of Interdisciplinary Humanities) 2, no. 1 (2005). http://iph.fsu.edu/interculture.

Lester, Joan. "The American Indian: A Museum's Eye View." *The Indian Historian* (Indian Historian Press, San Francisco) 5, no. 2 (1972).

Lippard, Lucy R. *Mixed Blessings: New Art in a Multicultural America.* New York: Pantheon Books, 1990.

———. "'Talking to Ourselves': Indian Art for Indian People." In *Bob Haozous, Indigenous Dialogue.* Santa Fe: Institute of American Indian Arts Museum, 2005.

Lowe, Truman T. "The Emergence of Native Modernism." In Lowe, *Native Modernism.*

———, ed. *Native Modernism: The Art of George Morrison and Allan Houser.* Washington, DC, and Seattle: National Museum of the American Indian, Smithsonian Institution, in association with University of Washington Press, 2004.

Lutz, Catherine, and Jane Collins. *Reading National Geographic.* Chicago: University of Chicago Press, 1993.

Mankiller, Wilma. *Every Day Is a Good Day: Reflections by Contemporary Indigenous Women.* Golden, CO: Fulcrum, 2004.

Martin, Lee-Ann. "Indigenous Renewal = Reclamation + Redefinition = Reality = Identity." In *16 Songs: Issues of Personal Assessment and Indigenous Renewal,* Diana R. Block and Edgar Heap of Birds. Denton, TX: University of North Texas Art Gallery, 1995.

McMaster, Gerald. "Living on Reservation X." In McMaster, *Reservation X.*

———. "New Art/New Contexts." Introduction to National Museum of the American Indian, *Vision, Space, Desire.*

———, ed. *Reservation X.* Seattle, WA, and Hull, Quebec: University of Washington Press and the Canadian Museum of Civilization, 1998.

McMaster, Gerald, and Lee-Ann Martin, eds. *Indigena: Contemporary Native Perspectives.* Hull, Quebec, and Vancouver, BC: Canadian Museum of Civilization and Douglas and McIntyre, 1992.

McNeil, Larry. Artist's statement in *Migrations: New Directions in Native American Art,* edited by Marjorie Devon. Albuquerque: University of New Mexico Press, 2006.

Mihesuah, Devon A. *Indigenous American Women.* Lincoln: University of Nebraska Press, 2003.

Miller, Angela, Janet Berlo, Bryan Wolf, and Jennifer Roberts. *American Encounters: Art, History and Cultural Identity.* New York: Prentice Hall, 2007.

Miller-Keller, Andrea. "Dunging the Ground." In *Hachivi Edgar Heap of Birds: MATRIX 131,* edited by Andrea Miller-Keller. Hartford, CT: Wadsworth Atheneum Museum of Art, 1996.

Mithlo, Nancy Marie. "Conspiracy Theory." In McMaster, *Reservation X.*

———. "'Give, Give, Giving': Cultural Translations." In National Museum of the American Indian, *Vision, Space, Desire.*

———. Review of *Staging the Indian: The Politics of Representation.* In *American Anthropologist* 105, no. 1 (March 2003): 156–61.

Mohanty, Satya P. "The Epistemic Status of Cultural Identity." In *Reclaiming Identity: Realist Theory and the Predicament of Postmodernism,* edited by Paula M. L. Moya and Michael R. Hames-Garcia. Berkeley: University of California Press, 2000.

Mundine, John. "Aboriginal Art in Australia Today." *Third Text* 6 (Spring 1989): 40–42.

Myers, Bernard S., ed. *McGraw-Hill Dictionary of Art.* New York: McGraw-Hill, 1969.

Naranjo-Morse, Nora. *Numbe Whageh (Our Center Place).* One videocassette (10 minutes), 2005; distributed by Vtape, Toronto.

National Museum of the American Indian. *Vision, Space, Desire: Global Perspectives and Cultural Hybridity.* Washington, DC: National Museum of the American Indian, Smithsonian Institution, 2006.

Nemiroff, Diana, Robert Houle, and Charlotte Townsend-Gault. *Land, Spirit, Power: First Nations at the National Gallery of Canada.* Ottawa: National Gallery of Canada, 1992.

Niro, Shelley. Artist's statement in *Staging the Indian: The Politics of Representation,* edited by Jill Sweet and Ian Berry. Saratoga Springs, NY: Tang Teaching Museum and Art Gallery at Skidmore College, 2002.

———. *Suite: INDIAN.* Videotape, 2005, distributed by Vtape, Toronto.

Oguibe, Olu. "In the Heart of Darkness." Quoted by Ery Camera in *A Fiction of Authenticity: Contemporary Africa Abroad,* edited by Shannon Fitzgerald and Tumelo Mosaka. St. Louis: Contemporary Art Museum, 2003.

Owens, Craig. "Improper Names." *Art in America,* October 1986.

Penney, David W. *North American Indian Art.* London: Thames & Hudson, 2004.

Pleshaw, Gregory. "Artistic Identity in Native America: What's in a Label?" *Santa Fe Trend,* Spring 2005.

Plumwood, Val. "Feminism and the Logic of Alterity." In *Representing Reason: Feminist Theory and Formal Logic,* edited by Rachel Joffe Falmagne and Majorie Hass. New York: Rowman & Littlefield, 2002.

Powers, William K. "Sacred Art and the Culturation of Nature." In *Beyond the Vision: Essays on American Indian Culture.* Norman, OK: University of Oklahoma Press, 1987.

Rickard, Jolene. "The Local and the Global." In National Museum of the American Indian, *Vision, Space, Desire.*

Rubinstein, Raphael. "A Quiet Crisis." *Art in America,* March 2003.

Rushing, W. Jackson, III. "Authenticity and Subjectivity in Post-War Painting: Concerning Herrera, Scholder, and Cannon." In Archuleta and Strickland, *Shared Visions.*

———. "In Our Language: The Emergence of Edgar Heap of Birds." *Third Text* 19 (July 2005): 365–84.

———. "The Legacy of Ledger Book Drawings in Twentieth-Century Native American Art." In Berlo, *Plains Indian Drawings, 1865–1935.*

———. "Street Chiefs and Native Hosts: Richard Ray (Whitman) and Edgar Heap of Birds Defend the Homeland." In *Green Acres: Neo-Colonialism in the United States,* edited by Christopher Scoates. St. Louis: Washington University Gallery of Art, 1992.

———, ed. *After the Storm: The Eiteljorg Fellowship for Native American Fine Art,* 2001. Indianapolis: Eiteljorg Museum of American Indians and Western Art, 2001.

———, ed. *Native American Art in the Twentieth Century.* New York: Routledge, 1999.

Ryan, Allan J. *The Trickster Shift: Humour and Irony in Contemporary Native Art.* Seattle: University of Washington Press, 1999.

Saltz, Jerry. "Seeing Out Loud: Having an Eye in Criticism Is as Important as Having an Ear in Music." *Village Voice,* December 16, 2005.

Smith, Paul Chaat. "Americans without Tears." In *No Reservations: Native American History and Culture in Contemporary Art.* Curated by Richard Klein with essays by Fergus M. Bordewich, Paul Chaat Smith, and Richard Klein. Ridgefield, CT: Aldrich Contemporary Art Museum, 2006.

———. "The Meaning of Life." In McMaster and Martin, *Indigena: Contemporary Native Perspectives.*

Spicer, Edward H. "Persistent Cultural Systems." *Science* 174, no. 4011 (1971): 795–800.

Strickland, Rennard. "Beyond the Ethnic Umbrella: Learning More about Contemporary Indian Painting and Sculpture." In *Magic Images: Contemporary Native American Art,* edited by Edwin Wade and Rennard Strickland. Norman, OK: Philbrook Art Center and University of Oklahoma Press, 1981.

Sullivan, Martin. Foreword to Archuleta and Strickland, *Shared Visions.*

Taussig, Michael. *Mimesis and Alterity: A Particular History of the Senses.* New York: Routledge, 1993.

Taylor, William E. Foreword to *"Bo'jou, Neejee!": Profiles of Canadian Indian Art,* by Ted Brasser. Ottawa: National Museum of Man, 1976.

Teather, J. Lynne. "Museum-Making in Canada (to 1972)." *Muse* (Canadian Museums Association, Ottawa), summer/fall 1992.

Todd, Loretta. "What More Do They Want?" In McMaster and Martin, *Indigena: Contemporary Native Perspectives.*

Townsend-Gault, Charlotte. "Let X=Audience." In McMaster, *Reservation X.*

———. "Translation or Perversion? Showing First Nations Art in Canada." *Cultural Studies* 9, no. 1 (1995): 91–105.

Tremblay, Gail. "Different Paths: Tracks Worth Following." In Lowe, *Native Modernism.*

Tsinhnahjinnie, Hulleah. In *Image and Self in Contemporary Native American Photoart.* Hanover, NH: Dartmouth College Hood Museum of Art, 1995.

Turney, Laura. "Ceci n'est pas Jimmie Durham." *Critique of Anthropology* 19, no. 4 (1999): 423–42.

van Alphen, Ernest. "The Other Within." In *Alterity, Identity, Image: Selves and Others in Society and Scholarship,* edited by Raymond Corbey and Joep Leerssen. Atlanta: Rodopi Press, 1991.

WalkingStick, Kay. "Native American Art in the Postmodern Era." *Art Journal* 51, no. 3 (Fall 1992): 15–17.

Young Man, Alfred. "The Metaphysics of North American Indian Art," In McMaster and Martin, *Indigena: Contemporary Native Perspectives.*

———. *Networking: Proceedings from National Native Indian Artists Symposium IV.* Lethbridge, Alberta: Privately published by Alfred Young Man, University of Lethbridge, 1988.

———. "The Socialization and Art Politics of Native Art." Ph.D. diss., Rutgers University. UMI Dissertation Services, Ann Arbor, MI, 1997.

Published in conjunction with the symposium "[Re]inventing the Wheel," at the Denver Art Museum, January 28, 2006.

Second printing, 2010.

Funding for "[Re]inventing the Wheel" was provided by an Economic Development Initiative grant made possible by former U.S. Senator Ben Nighthorse Campbell with additional funding provided by the citizens who support the Scientific and Cultural Facilities District. Publication and distribution of this book were generously underwritten by the Ford Foundation with the support and encouragement of Elizabeth Theobald Richards.

Front and Back Cover: *Wheel,* 2005
Edgar Heap of Birds
Porcelain on steel, diam. 50 ft.

Frontispiece: *Corn Blue Room,* 1998
Jolene K. Rickard
Mixed media installation, 12 × 20 × 15 ft.

Library of Congress Cataloging-in-Publication Data
   [Re]inventing the wheel : advancing the dialogue on contemporary American Indian art / Nancy J. Blomberg, editor.
     p. cm.
   Published in conjunction with the symposium "[Re]inventing the wheel," at the Denver Art Museum, Jan. 28, 2006.
   Includes bibliographical references.
   ISBN 978-0-914738-59-6 (softcover : alk. paper)
   1. Indian art—United States—20th century—Congresses.
2. Art, American—20th century—Congresses.  I. Blomberg, Nancy J., 1946–. II. Denver Art Museum. III. Title: Reinventing the wheel.
N6538.A4R45 2008
704.03'97—dc22                       2008029624

Published and distributed by Denver Art Museum
  www.denverartmuseum.org

General editor: Nancy J. Blomberg
Copyedited by Laura Caruso
Proofread by John Pierce and Marie Weiler
Designed by John Hubbard
Typeset by Brynn Warriner
Color management by iocolor, Seattle
Produced by Marquand Books, Inc., Seattle
  www.marquand.com
Printed and bound in China by 1010 Printing International, Ltd.